ANCIENTS AND MODERNS

General Editor: Phiroze Vasunia, Reader in Classics, University of Reading

How can antiquity illuminate critical issues in the modern world? How does the ancient world help us address contemporary problems and issues? In what ways do modern insights and theories shed new light on the interpretation of ancient texts, monuments, artefacts and cultures? The central aim of this exciting new series is to show how antiquity is relevant to life today. The series also points towards the ways in which the modern and ancient worlds are mutually connected and interrelated. Lively, engaging, and historically informed, *Ancients and Moderns* examines key ideas and practices in context. It shows how societies and cultures have been shaped by ideas and debates that recur. With a strong appeal to students and teachers in a variety of disciplines, including classics and ancient history, each book is written for non-specialists in a clear and accessible manner.

PAGE duBOIS is Distinguished Professor of Classics and Comparative Literature at the University of California, San Diego. Her many books include *Torture and Truth* (1991), *Sappho is Burning* (1997), *Trojan Horses. Saving Classics from the Conservatives* (2001) and *Slaves and other Objects* (2003).

ANCIENTS AND MODERN SERIES

THE ART OF THE BODY: ANTIQUITY AND ITS LEGACY • MICHAEL SQUIRE

DEATH: ANTIQUITY AND ITS LEGACY • MARIO ERASMO

DRAMA: ANTIQUITY AND ITS LEGACY • DAVID ROSENBLOOM

GENDER: ANTIQUITY AND ITS LEGACY • BROOKE HOLMES

LUCK, FATE AND FORTUNE: ANTIQUITY AND ITS LEGACY • ESTHER EIDINOW

MAGIC AND DEMONS: ANTIQUITY AND ITS LEGACY • TO BE ANNOUNCED

MEDICINE: ANTIQUITY AND ITS LEGACY • CAROLINE PETIT

PHILOSOPHY: ANTIQUITY AND ITS LEGACY • EMILY WILSON

POLITICS: ANTIQUITY AND ITS LEGACY • KOSTAS VLASSOPOULOS

RACE: ANTIQUITY AND ITS LEGACY • DENISE MCCOSKEY

RELIGION: ANTIQUITY AND ITS LEGACY • TO BE ANNOUNCED

SEX: ANTIQUITY AND ITS LEGACY • DANIEL ORRELLS

SLAVERY: ANTIQUITY AND ITS LEGACY • PAGE DUBOIS

SPORT: ANTIQUITY AND ITS LEGACY • PAUL CHRISTESEN

WAR: ANTIQUITY AND ITS LEGACY • TO BE ANNOUNCED

ANCIENTS AND MODERNS

SLAVERY
ANTIQVITY AND
ITS LEGACY

PAGE duBOIS

OXFORD
UNIVERSITY PRESS

OXFORD
UNIVERSITY PRESS

Oxford University Press, Inc., publishes works that further Oxford University's objective of excellence in research, scholarship, and education.

Oxford New York Auckland Cape Town Dar es Salaam Hong Kong Karachi Kuala Lumpur
Madrid Melbourne Mexico City Nairobi New Delhi Shanghai Taipei Toronto

With offices in
Argentina Austria Brazil Chile Czech Republic France Greece Guatemala Hungary Italy
Japan Poland Portugal Singapore South Korea Switzerland Thailand Turkey
Ukraine Vietnam

First published by I.B.Tauris & Co. Ltd. in the United Kingdom

Published by Oxford University Press, Inc.
198 Madison Avenue, New York, New York 10016

www.oup.com

Oxford is a registered trademark of Oxford University Press

DuBois, Page.
Slavery ancient and modern : antiquity and its legacy / by Page Dubois.
p. cm. – (Ancients and moderns)
ISBN 978-0-19-538084-2 – ISBN 978-0-19-538085-9
1. Slavery. 2. Slavery–History. I. Title.
HT861.D83 2009
306.3'6209--dc22   2009034704

Typeset in Garamond Pro by Ellipsis Books Limited, Glasgow
Printed and bound in Great Britain by CPI Antony Rowe, Chippenham

To John

CONTENTS

PREFACE

Slavery has been part of human societies from time immemorial, for as long as human beings have dominated, coerced, and owned one another. Although we might hope that slavery has now vanished from an enlightened world, this is not the case. In this book, I consider the presence of slaves in the present, and the relationship between the ancient past of slavery and its present. This is a story filled not just with shock and suffering, but also with the intimacy between slave owners and slaves. And with the amazing resilience and resistance at times exhibited by the many millions of slaves who have lived through the historical period of human history, many anonymous and forgotten. Like any book written on the subject of slavery now, the engagement is directed toward abolition, toward a final end to human beings' ownership of one another. But this book also seeks to look back at the authority of antiquity, the ways in which ancient institutions of slavery offered models not just of domination, but also of resistance to the violence, social death and dishonour of enslavement.

The vast scholarship on living slaves, on racialised slavery, on ancient slavery, on films concerning slavery, can only be hinted at in a short book like the present one. I have tried, rather than to cover exhaustively all the issues, the controversies, the scholarly debates about the relationship between ancient and modern slavery, to call up some of the voices of the slaves, when we have access to them, and to privilege the words of masters and slaves if possible. I have indicated those works of scholarship that I have found most helpful, without trying to present full bibliographies on these great questions.

I go backwards in time, from the present, to the recent past, the early modern, and then to antiquity, and end with some recent cinematic representations of slavery in antiquity. Chapter 1, 'Living Slaves,' contains accounts of some of the millions of people enslaved in the world today. I rely on such scholarly work as Kevin Bales' *Disposable People*; he offers a sweeping portrait of slavery across a huge geographical area, and includes domestic, industrial, agricultural, and sexual slaves in the current situation of globalization. There are journalists' accounts, also, of criminal cases filed against enslavers; one from the *Los Angeles Times* of October 24, 2006, begins: 'An Irvine couple who pleaded guilty to enslaving a 10-year-old Egyptian girl were sentenced to federal prison Monday.., ' (B7) Chapter 2, 'Racialised Slavery,' moves from the slaves of today to the early modern and modern institution of the enslavement of Africans, in which 'Moors' and eventually, people of colour, became the preferred targets of slavery in the context of early capitalism. Chapter 3, 'Ancient Ideologies,' reviews the arguments concerning slavery, from the situation of slaves in the Hebrew Bible, the ancient Greeks' debates on slavery, to Aristotle's views on natural slavery, to readings of the New Testament writings of Paul, to modern thinkers who thought the New World should emulate the old in providing leisure for freedom of thought and political action for the master class, by ensuring that labour was performed by slaves. Here too are sources for abolitionist thinkers. Chapter 4, 'Ancient Slavery,' offers a picture of ancient slavery based on textual and material evidence. A particular focus is the place of slaves in the earliest comedy in the Western tradition, in the work of Aristophanes, Plautus and Terence, himself a freed slave. Is the figure of a despised yet wily underling crucial to the invention and survival of comedy, and to the slavemasters' acceptance of slavery, their sense of relief in laughter at their possessions' antics? The last chapter, on twentieth-century representations of slavery in the ancient world, takes up not only the new industry of 'thanatourism,' so-called 'hospitality' sites that invite tourists to visit locations associated with slavery in the past. I also look at cinematic representations of slavery, especially in the case of the ancient Israelites, and ancient Roman slaves. This chapter looks at *The Ten*

Commandments, which depicts the liberation of the ancient Israelites from captivity and enslavement, the film *Spartacus*, made in the wake of the McCarthyist era by some of the Hollywood Ten, representing a famous slave rebellion, and the more recent *Gladiator*, also featuring a revolt, albeit by a single slave. The very different interpretations of ancient slavery in these three films point to the constantly mutating relationship between any present and antiquity, and to the possibilities of an endlessly productive critical engagement with the past.

CHAPTER 1

LIVING SLAVES

This is the voice of Christine, a sex slave born in the state of Minnesota in the United States of America, in 1968:

> I was born into a prostitution ring, a family of pimps and porno-graphers and prostitutes. . . . In prostitution rings women and girls are taught to be sexually submissive by men who refer to themselves as masters . . . the men are masters of torture and terror who are highly trained in torture techniques . . . They want us to feel utterly powerless . . . to feel dead, look dead, be dead. Above all else, they want us immobilized. They want to consume our lives, take our freedom with no resistance whatsoever. . . . I wanted to not be sold. I wanted to not be bought.[1]

Her account comes from a volume of contemporary slave narratives compiled by Kevin Bales and Zoe Trodd, which reveals the terrible extent of the institution of slavery in the present, an institution that most people living in our globalizing, postmodern world assume was abolished for good in the nineteenth century.

This is a passage from an ancient Athenian forensic oration by Lysias, from the fourth century BCE, recorded in the voice of a slave owner who was accused of wounding, with premeditation, another Athenian, over the possession of a slave woman whom they owned jointly. This text derives from a context often idealized in Western political theory and philosophy,

1

the ancient city of Athens, the *polis* in which were invented democracy, philosophy, the jury trial, much that Western civilization holds dear, claims as its own and often seeks to export to or impose on other civilizations in the present. The centrality of the institution of slavery in the ancient Greek city, and in the Roman empire, is often overlooked. But this legal speech reveals a situation similar to that of Christine, born in 1968 CE. The wounded accuser of the fourth century BCE, bringing the speaker to trial, had apparently argued, in another speech now lost to us, that he alone was the owner of the slave; the speaker defends himself:

> [My opponent] denies, in face of the settlement clearly made on every point, that we agreed to share the woman between us. (Lysias 4. 1–2)[2]
> . . . we admit that we went to see boys and flute-girls and were in liquor . . . (4.7)
> As to her, sometimes it is I, and sometimes he, for whom she professes affection, wishing to be loved by both. (4. 8)

The two men, according to the speaker, each put down an equal sum of money in order to own this woman jointly:

> It would be far more just to have her tortured for the purpose of this charge than to have her sold . . . It is your duty, therefore, [he says to the male, citizen jurors] to reject his claim that the woman should not be tortured, which he made on the pretended ground of her freedom. (4.14)
> In having her put to the torture I must be at a disadvantage, and yet I ran this grave risk; for clearly she was much more attached to him than to me, and has joined him in wronging me. (4. 17)

As always with evidence from antiquity concerning slaves, we have only the voice of the master, never a slave narrative spoken by the slave herself. Yet this woman emerges briefly from the shadows in this speech – owned by two men simultaneously, pulled between the two, vulnerable to torture in the Athenian court system, which allowed testimony from slaves only if it was obtained through torture. We cannot hear her voice, yet register her presence through the symptomatic speech of one of her owners, even her attempt, perhaps, to avoid torture and win freedom by manipulating these two men, finding one more sympathetic than the other. In the ancient case, slavery is completely legal; it is the wounding, the throwing of a potsherd by one owner at the other, that is at stake in the court case, and that requires the torture of the slave. In the case of Christine of Minnesota, her enslavement is illegal, and it is those who illegally possessed her as a slave who tortured her. Yet we can see parallels between these two women, far distant as they are in time, one living in the fifth century BCE, the other 2500 years later. One is implicated in the imperial world of ancient Athens, the other in the centre of a new empire, that of a post-national, newly global Empire with a capital E.

There are many slaves living in the present, in highly varied circumstances, doing domestic labour, working in industries, in agriculture and in the sex trade. These slaves fall into the hands of their owners in various ways through birth, as in the case of Christine of Minnesota. Sometimes they are sold by their families, who cannot support them or themselves without the income from sale. Others are kidnapped or captured by slave agents; some, as a last resort, sell themselves. Some are tricked into believing they are leaving some unsatisfactory situation to make a new life, with a new form of employment in a strange country, and find themselves trapped in slavery from which they cannot extricate themselves.

Slavery Defined

What is slavery? Historians and scholars who study slavery in the past and present offer differing definitions of the condition commonly known as slavery. For some, it is simply the state of being owned by another, being the property of another human being. This can be a permanent or a temporary condition, but in either case the freedom of the enslaved individual is curtailed entirely, and, through the threat of force and even death, the slave must obey her or his master. Some scholars argue that, in fact, the term slavery should be reserved for those falling permanently into this condition, and that other forms of indentured labour, of possession that has a limit, should not be called slavery. A dictionary definition: 'bondage to a master or household.'[3] Becky Cornell, and Kevin Bales, one of the most active and prolific abolitionists at work today, present this definition in their book *Slavery Today*:

> Slavery is a social and economic relationship in which a person is controlled through violence or the threat of violence, is paid nothing, and is economically exploited.[4]

One of the most useful and compelling recent definitions of slavery comes from the sociologist Orlando Patterson, whose book *Slavery and Social Death: A Comparative Study*, published in 1982, has had great impact on the historical and contemporary study of slavery.[5] His definition focuses not on the fact of possession by another but rather on the life circumstances of an enslaved person:

> slavery is the permanent, violent domination of natally alienated and generally dishonoured persons. (13)

In some respects, Patterson's work on comparative world historical slavery offers an important corrective to economistic or legal definitions of slavery, and is rather an 'immanent' definition, one that reads the condition of the slave from inside his or her experience. He calls slavery 'a relation of domination,' and argues that slavery is distinctive as a relation of domination. In his view, power relations, relations of domination, have three facets: first, the social, entailing the use or threat of violence in the control of one person by another; second, the psychological facet of influence, the capacity to persuade another person to change the way he perceives his interests and his circumstances and, third, the cultural facet of authority, transforming force into right, obedience into duty. The specificity of slavery in regard to other relationships of domination resides in its particular manifestations: first, that in relation to the social, slavery exhibits an extremity of power and of coercion, in its use of direct violence, where slavery itself is a substitute for violent death. Secondly, slavery is 'natal alienation.' The slave is a 'socially dead' person, a genealogical isolate. And, third, for the slave, 'dishonour' becomes a generalized condition. The slave is thus the victim of extremes of coercion and violence, suffering the equivalent of death, becomes socially dead and dwells in a state of absolute dishonour. Through these categories Patterson engages in a great mapping of the whole that is the history of world slavery, discerning 'patterns' in a cross-cultural, transhistorical survey. His vocabulary relies on some of the categories of Marxism, and he touches on questions of power, contradiction, and Hegel's dialectic of lord and bondsman, or 'master and slave,' dominator and dominated. He discusses in some detail such questions as the four basic features of the 'ritual of enslavement:' 'first, the symbolic rejection by the slave of his past and his former kinsmen; second, a change of name; third, the imposition of some visible mark of servitude; and, last, the assumption of a new status in the household or economic organization of the master.' (52) It is interesting that when Frederick Douglass, the famed abolitionist ex-slave of nineteenth-century America, escapes to freedom, he is convinced by an abolitionist friend in New Bedford to keep the name Frederick, given him by his mother, saying 'I must hold on to that, to preserve a sense of my identity'[6]

In a later work, somewhat controversial, Patterson argues that the category of freedom, so important to traditions of Western philosophy, could emerge only in the conditions of the Greek polis, that with the emphasis on citizen freedom in the Greek city-state the category of unfreedom, of enslavement, helped to generate, by contrast, the characterization of freedom in the citizen class.[7] In disagreement with Isaiah Berlin's claim that the notion of personal liberty is 'comparatively modern,' Patterson locates it in antiquity: 'freedom was generated from the experience of slavery. People came to value freedom, to construct it as a powerful shared vision of life, as a result of their experience of, and response to, slavery or its recombinant form, serfdom, in their roles as masters, slaves, and non-slaves.'[8] This view is controversial in part because Patterson argues that the idea of freedom does not have such power outside the West, that 'non-Western peoples have thought so little about freedom that most human languages did not even possess a word for the concept before contact with the West.' (x) His argument here can be seen to contribute to an idealization of Western civilization, a celebration of its superiority, and of course, a justification for colonialism and imperialism. But these are issues for another book.

I would like, in this book, to hold the several definitions of 'slavery' in tension with one another, to see the relationship of bondage as central to the condition of slaves, but also keep in mind the focus on the subjectivity of the slave him or herself, the ways in which slaves, at various moments in history or in differing geographical locations, share the fate of implicit or enacted violence, social death and a life lived in dishonour.[9] It is crucial to remember these features of slaves' subjectivity and experience, especially with regard to ancient slaves, whose own testimony about their lives is rarely available, except in such mediated forms as the work of Epiktetos, a freed slave, and the fabulist Aesop, himself allegedly a freed slave, whose work was probably not the product of a single author, but a collection of stories repeated and associated with his name.[10]

Numbers and Places

How many slaves live in the world today? Kevin Bales and Becky Cornell estimate that there are at present twenty-seven million, scattered throughout the world, with the majority living in South Asia. There are, however, many slaves in Southeast Asia, in Brazil and elsewhere in South America, in North and Western Africa and in every country in the world. (*ST*, 8) Christine of Minnesota, cited at the beginning of this chapter, is not an exception; slaves in the United States and in Britain include not only Americans born into slavery, but also others 'trafficked,' deceived into slavery through promises of work, and volunteering to immigrate only to be enslaved.

E. Benjamin Skinner tells the story of Rambho Kumar, born in the poor state of Bihar, in India, and sold at nine-years old, by his mother, for 700 rupees ($15) to a carpet-maker.[11] The owner made him and his fellow-slaves work nineteen hours a day, and when the boy injured himself at the loom, the slave-holder would cauterize his wound by sticking his finger into boiling oil. When the boys tried to run away, the owner would track them down and beat them. Skinner defines slaves as 'those who are forced to work, under threat of violence, for no pay beyond subsistence.' (M10) He makes a distinction between prostitution, which in his view may be voluntary, not-coerced, and slavery, although some others argue that there is no such thing as the voluntary choice of prostitution. He argues that the Bush administration erred in focusing on the ending of prostitution world-wide, rather than on the abolition of slavery, since 'more than 90% of modern-day slaves are not held in commercial sexual slavery.' The description of sexual slaves, enslaved to perform acts of prostitution, has an inflammatory quality, especially for Americans, that can lead to abolitionist action, but, in fact, most slaves in the world today are not trafficked for sexual purposes, but rather for labour.

The Poetics of Slavery

Another slave narrative, recorded in 1996, comes from Seba, from Mali:

> I was raised by my grandmother in Mali, and when I was still a little girl, a woman my family knew came and asked her if she could take me to Paris to care for her children . . . Every day I started work before 7 A.M. and finished about 11 P.M. . . . She often beat me . . . She beat me with the broom, with kitchen tools, or whipped me with an electric cable . . . Once . . . my mistress and her husband . . . beat and then threw me out on the street. I had nowhere to go. (*Slavery Today*, 98)

Seba wanders the streets, cannot communicate with anyone, finally is taken back to the house, beaten some more and thereafter always locked in the apartment. This form of trafficking occurs frequently; the promises of labour in another country, or another region of the same country, turn into bondage, slavery, as the person transferred from family to a new situation finds that there is no escape, no compensation, no recourse and . . . often, because of an illegal immigration situation, cannot appeal for help to the authorities.

The condition of enslavement enters into the literary record of the twentieth and twenty-first centuries. The narrative of Seba connects with the novel *Le Devoir de Violence*, in Kwame Anthony Appiah's term a 'post-realist' text published in Paris in 1968 by Yambo Ouologuem.[12] The Malian author introduces his hero, after reaching back into the history of his people:

> The life that Raymond lived . . . was the life of his whole generation
> – the first generation of native administrators maintained by the
> notables in a state of gilded prostitution – rare merchandise, dark
> genius manoeuvered behind the scenes and hurled into the tempests
> of colonial politics amidst the hot smell of festivities and machina-
> tions – ambiguous balancing acts in which the master turned the
> slave into the first of the slaves and the arrogant equal of the white
> master, and in which the slave thought himself master of the master,
> who himself had fallen to the level of the first of the slaves. . . . (136)

The sister of the hero has undergone enslavement; he leaves her behind in Africa, but then, when he goes to Paris and encounters a prostitute, he learns this is his sister, who has fallen into bondage in the metropolis. From her he learns that his fiancée is dead, his father has been sold, and that his two brothers had been drugged and went mad. Brother and sister weep together and then:

> A week later Raymond, taking advantage of Sunday to visit his sister,
> was told that a sadistic customer had concealed a razor blade in the
> soap on Kadidia's bidet and that in washing herself she had cut herself
> so deeply that the haemorrhage had drained her blood and killed her
> before help could come. (147)

8

Kadidia dies in the brothel. When he finds a male lover, his memory goes back to his homeland: 'his search was not so much for ecstasy as for the profound meaning of his own destruction, the stain on his face suddenly splattered by his name: Spartacus!' (156) After he returns home: 'he himself was a problematic existence, a living conflict. In this alienation, to be sure, Raymond-Spartacus Kassoumi found an open door to revolt: for him and his Africa it was in a sense a duty to be revolutionary. But how . . .?' (168) Even as the contradictions and ironies of the relationship between Africa and France, and within Mali itself, lead him to an endless round of alienation, the name Spartacus obliges him to violence, to revolutionary action like his imaginary ancestor's, to be discussed in Chapter Five.

Slavery in the Media

Of course slavery in Africa persists. In the New York Times of 28 October 2008, there appeared a news story with the headline: 'Court Rules Niger Failed By Allowing Girl's Slavery.'[13] The account, filed from Dakar in Senegal, reports that the government of Niger 'had failed to protect a young woman sold into slavery at the age of 12.' A regional tribunal sitting for the first time in Niamey, capital of Niger, ordered the government to pay damages to the woman, twenty-four years old at the time of the judgment. She had been born into 'a traditional slave class', sold for about five hundred dollars, forced to work in her owner's fields for ten years and raped repeatedly. She sued the Niger government on the grounds that it had failed to enforce its own anti-slavery laws. She had already been imprisoned for bigamy, having married although her master claimed that he was her husband. The victor in the lawsuit Hadijatou Mani issued a statement after the judgment: 'Nobody deserves to be enslaved.' The reporter further noted, as background to this story, that 'Antislavery organizations estimate that 43,000 people are enslaved in Niger alone, where nomadic tribes like the Tuareg and Toubou have for centuries held members of other ethnic groups as slaves.'

The New York Times, on 3 December 2007, reported another case of what it called 'Modern-Day Slavery,' this time on Long Island, in the suburbs of New York City. Two Indonesian women had served as 'live-in help' by a couple, naturalized citizens from India, who were on trial for 'involuntary servitude and peonage, or, in the common national parlance since 1865, the crime of keeping slaves.'[14] The reporter recalls, in this story, another instance, a conviction in Boston in 2006 of 'the wife of a Saudi prince' found guilty of 'keeping two house servants for three years in virtual slavery.' A Brazilian couple was convicted in 2003; they 'kept a Brazilian woman in their home as a servant for 15 years, paying her nothing.' In this story, the reporter notes that the number of such victims is difficult to ascertain, and of course the indictments and convictions may represent only the tip of an iceberg of slavery in the United States today, but estimates suggest that 'people trafficked to the United States annually' are 15,000 to 20,000, and that about a third of those trafficked end up as domestic workers. In the Long Island case, the women were forced to sleep in their owners' 'multimillion-dollar home,' laboured night and day, and were tortured and beaten, malnourished, and prevented from leaving their place of enslavement except when they were carrying out the garbage. The prosecutor in this case noted how difficult it was to arrive at prosecution and conviction in such cases, citing 'language and cultural barriers,' depression and simple fear. The case in question was one of about one hundred prosecutions for involuntary servitude since passage of an anti-trafficking law in the year 2000.

Such newspaper accounts are common in the United States, and attempt to bring the problem of human trafficking to public attention. E. Benjamin Skinner, in an article in the *Los Angeles Times* Opinion section of 23 March 2008, points to what he calls the 'staying power' of slavery in the present:

In a rundown mansion in a slum of Bucharest, Romania, a pimp offered to sell me a young woman he described as 'a blonde.' She had bleached hair, hastily applied makeup, and she apparently suffered from Down syndrome. On her right arm were at least 10 angry, fresh slashes where, I can only assume, she has attempted suicide.

10

The pimp claimed that he made 200 euros per night renting her out to local clients. He offered to sell her outright to me in exchange for a used car.

Slavery and 'Race'

One of the most vexed issues concerning slavery in the present is the question of race, racialisation, and the vulnerability of minorities to enslavement not only by residents of the metropolis, but by their own neighbours and fellow-citizens. There is a complex nexus of issues of class, inherited class status and racialisation here. As will become clear in the chapters that follow, the racialisation of slavery is a feature that marks early modern and modern slavery. While the masters of ancient Greece and Rome did not often have slaves of other so-called 'races,' for example, African slaves from Nubia, they did make a distinction at times between the 'naturally' enslaved barbarians, and their fellow citizens. The arguments made by such theorists of slavery as Aristotle in this regard paved the way for the racialised slavery of the early modern and modern periods, where millions of Africans were captured, kidnapped, and transported across the Atlantic as slaves. There are other issues of inherited status, of minorities and of class, which also enter the picture of contemporary slavery.

Kevin Bales argues that 'race' is no longer an issue in contemporary slavery, and that this fact makes the argument for abolition more likely to succeed than at earlier periods. This is a much-disputed claim, one that rests on shaky evidence, in my opinion. Although it is true, for example, that whole villages are enslaved in Northern India, and that the slaves in these villages are not 'racially' differentiated from those who deploy them as masters, the divide between the global South and the North is an important one in mapping the extent and specificities of slavery now. Differences that do not rise to the level of 'racial' differences, even in the eyes of those involved, can have their impact on who is born into slavery, who is captured and made a slave, who is trafficked as a volunteer into slavery. Religious questions, religious differences of caste or different cults can have consequences on who becomes a slave, who a master. If the Arab descendants of the janjaweed in Africa conquer, subjugate, enslave or drive into bondage the indigenous African peoples of Darfur, then race, as a perceived difference, does have effects on the shape of slavery in the present.

If the global South is as a whole indebted, impoverished and driven off traditionally owned lands, as Bales himself describes, then the question of racialisation does figure in our view of global slavery. He points out that war, debt and the absence of legal institutions provide ripe opportunity for the enslavement of endangered populations. In the case of Yugoslavia, for example, the Balkan state once governed as a whole by Marshall Tito, that fell into ethnic states at war with one another after his death, we saw the enslavement of people who had taken for granted their privileged status as citizens of Europe, governed by law and guaranteed sustenance and legal protections. The conflict among former citizens of Yugoslavia, classified in terms of ethnic, even racial differences, over-determined by religious distinctions and class, produced the enslavement of women, in particular, in a pattern that has been visible also in the aftermath of chaotic circumstances in the former republics of the Soviet Union.

Abolition: Or, What is to be Done?

What can we make of the call to abolish slavery in the present? Bales acknowledges, as an argument for abolition, that: 'The actual monetary value of slavery in the world economy is extremely small, a tiny fraction of the global economy. The end of slavery does not threaten the livelihood of any country or industry.'[15] In *Not for Sale: The Return of the Global Slave Trade—and How We Can Fight It*, David Batstone urges a personal response to the problem: 'I am convinced that every single individual can make a valuable contribution to arrest the global slave trade. If you doubt that fact, it is probably because you underestimate the power of your personal resources.'[16] Yet, Bales argues that such practices as boycotting goods from regions that have some slave labour, such as cotton or cocoa, may in fact have consequences damaging to those who employ free labour in these same regions. The numbers of slaves are so small in relation to the total production of many of these goods, that a boycott would have a deleterious effect on trade, force small employers out of business and make their labourers vulnerable to enslavement. Bales argues for government intervention and praises, for example, the efforts of the current Brazilian administration. As a former worker and labour organizer, the president of Brazil has set up a few mobile inspection teams, with mobile courts that can try slave-holders in the regions in which they predominate, for example in the charcoal producing areas of Western Amazonian Brazil. Although their numbers are small and convictions and liberations few, Bales sees this as an important step. Since all nations now have laws against slavery, abolition must rest on enforcement rather than on the passage of legislation. He also argues for donation to non-governmental organizations such as Free the Slaves, or its European sister organization, Anti-Slavery International, which send community organizers called liberators into villages such as those in Northern India populated entirely by slaves. Slaves are more visible and more accessible in such circumstances, and organizers can persuade slaves to take the risks of defying their masters and extricating themselves from slavery. But Bales also stresses the necessity for support as former slaves leave their conditions of bondage. As will become clear in Chapter 2, slaves who are suddenly removed from enslavement without economic support or training can easily fall into new forms of social death, as happened in the long and terrible story of African Americans enslaved in the rural south both before and after the civil war.[17]

The work of the non-governmental organizations such as Free the Slaves is admirable. These are compassionate, virtuous, admirable efforts, but they do not address the global economy in which slavery is now embedded. Along with other political theorists of the present, Jacques Rancière, in *Disagreement*, condemns humanitarianism, the sorts of efforts that might result in non-governmental organizations' attempts to address the question of slavery, and to eradicate it from the world of the present:

The age of the 'humanitarian' is one of immediate identity between the ordinary example of suffering humanity and the plenitude of the subject of humanity and of its rights. The eligible party pure and simple is then none other than the wordless victim, the ultimate figure of the one excluded from the logos, armed only with a voice expressing a monotonous moan, the moan of naked suffering, which saturation has made inaudible. More precisely, this person who is merely human then boils down to the couple of the victim, the pathetic figure of a person to whom such humanity is denied, and the executioner, the monstrous figure of a person who denies humanity.[18]

This, for Jacques Ranciere, is not 'politics,' and cannot respond to the structural wrongs of the present.

Giorgio Agamben, like Ranciere, sees the limits of humanitarianism, claiming that it reduces those in refugee camps, for example, to 'bare life,' a purely animal existence, and keeps them there, attending only to their bare life needs.

The separation between humanitarianism and politics that we are experiencing today is the extreme phase of the separation of the rights of man from the rights of the citizen. In the final analysis, however, humanitarian organizations – which today are more and more supported by international commissions – can only grasp human life in the figure of bare or sacred life and, therefore, despite themselves, maintain a secret solidarity with the very powers they ought to fight. . . . The 'imploring eyes' of the Rwandan child . . . may well be the most telling contemporary cipher of the bare life that humanitarian organizations, in perfect symmetry with state power, need. A humanitarianism separated from politics cannot fail to reproduce the isolation of sacred life at the basis of sovereignty, and the camp – which is to say, the pure space of exception – is the biopolitical paradigm that it cannot master.[19]

Although the slaves described in the collections of narratives now available do not reside in refugee camps, they are nonetheless subject to rescue efforts that, though useful and valuable, need to be supported by more radical schemes of transformation, by governments or by international groups like labour unions. Alain Badiou, too, in his critique of relativism, particulars and 'victimism,' similarly condemns the paralysis and inaudibility of groups tended by humanitarian impulses.[20]

This may be a peculiarly French issue, given the history of 'Médecins sans Frontières' and the inclusion of Bernard Kouchner in the cabinet of Nicolas Sarkozy. Yet it touches on the global as well. The sensationalization of sex slavery in particular caters to a certain public. The *New York Times* columnist Nicholas Kristof catalogues the tragic circumstances of sexual slaves in Southeast Asia, writes about them feelingly, and appeals not only to feminist indignation, but perhaps also to a semi-pornographic liberalism. The American cable network MSNBC aired an on-going series on sex slaves which similarly points to terrible suffering, but which spectacularizes and pornographizes it, so that viewers are encouraged to congratulate themselves on their goodwill and horror at what is portrayed, while never coming to an analysis of why such traffic is sustained in the current situation.

Both Batstone's and Cornell and Bales's books recount the narrative of a humanitarian effort gone wrong, an effort by Christians to rescue Africans which resulted in further bondage and suffering. This is the story of Given Kachepa, a Zambian boy who was recruited by a group called Teaching Teachers to Teach, to sing in a choir, and to come to the United States and raise money, through concerts, for school-building back in Zambia, while himself receiving an education in the USA. Pastor Grimes persuaded Zambian officials to grant visas to the boys and to falsify their ages on their passports, so that they would appear to be even younger than they were, and thus more marvelous. But when the boys arrived in Texas, they were awakened at dawn every day and forced to dig, by hand, a swimming pool. Later, on tour, they worked eighteen hours a day, every day of the week, for weeks at a time, traveling from concert to concert.

Given had his heart set on an education, and so three months into his US stay he asked Pastor Grimes and his daughter, Barbara Grimes Martens, when the boys' tutoring might begin. They passed into an angry frenzy, screaming at Given, even swearing at him, for being so ungrateful for the opportunity to live in America.[21]

After the pastor died, his daughter and her husband continued to manage the Zambian boys' choir, sending none of the money earned by the choir back to Zambia, and eventually tried to have two of them, guilty of trouble-making, deported by the Immigration and Naturalization Service. Finally, their bondage was exposed, and they were rescued from their enslavement.

Slavery in the present *is* a monstrous feature of contemporary global-ization; Kevin Bales, who has done much important work on this matter, wrote: 'There are more slaves alive today than all the people stolen from Africa at the time of the transatlantic slave trade.'[22] Yet the campaigns against slavery rest on liberal assumptions, disregard questions of racialised slavery, and the role of globalization in the perpetuation of slavery into the present. Bales, for example, writes, 'In the new slavery, race means little.' (10) Much of the public discourse concerning abolition of slavery in the present presents slave narratives as records of victimization, and calls for empathy, donations to international charitable organizations, the reduction, essentially, of the enslaved to *homines sacri*, to use Agamben's term, barely alive, without any recognition of the partial nature of the remedy being proposed. Like the appeals to those who sympathize with animals, and who are called upon to contribute to the World Wildlife Fund through the representation in television ads of pathetically impris-oned animals, the call for money permits a self-congratulatory comfort for the donor, who need not question his or her assumptions about the structural inequalities in the global economy, in which some are indeed disposable, exploited as slaves or in the equivalent of slavery subjected to 'necropolitics' rather than biopolitics. The call for the abolition of slavery in these circumstances, in the new empires, in the new Empire, is not a utopian demand. It is a call for emancipation of all, a necessary element of enlightenment and universalism, but it cannot go far enough in offering a critique of the economic and social arrangements of the present, in calling for real transformation.

The question of redemption also arises in the context of the call for an end to slavery in the present. Redemption, a term which has mystical and metaphysical connotations, also refers to the practice of buying slaves out of slavery, and freeing them. It has been used in Africa to free enslaved persons, and money has been raised in the US, especially by Christian charitable groups, to purchase and then free people enslaved. Many, however, see this practice as problematic. It profits the slave-traders, and therefore seems not to address the problem of trading in any way, and in fact may encourage more enslavement for more profit. In addition, there seems to be little support for those who have been liberated from slavery, and who are in danger, without any economic resources, of falling back into slavery. Some have argued those bought out of slavery may deceptively represent themselves as enslaved once again, and share the cost of their redemption with the alleged slave traders themselves.

Differences

In an article in the *New York Times Magazine*, the professor of philosophy at Princeton University, Kwame Anthony Appiah, discussed the issue of slavery in Ghana, where he was raised. He recalls hearing of the great Ashanti empire and its flourishing from the seventeenth century onwards, but remembers little mention of the slave trade in which it was engaged, exporting slaves to the Americas, many from farther east in Africa. And he noted that the legacy of slavery endures in Ghana, that people descended from slaves, long after slavery had been legally abolished, remained marked by their families' past. He recalls visits to his father from villagers, when he was a child: 'The village had belonged, I was told, to my father's family, and he inherited responsibility for it when he became the head of the family.' (16) There were plantations, villages of the descendants of slaves:

17

In the slaving empire of Ashanti, as the Ghanaian historian Akosua Perbi tells us, there were different designations for different kinds of forced labourers – war captives (who could, if they were lucky, be redeemed by the payment of ransom), people held as security for their families' debts, people bought at the slave markets elsewhere and family servants with a status akin to feudal serfs—[23]

Appiah watched his father try to refuse the role of judge the descendants of such slaves still granted him, as he accepted their gifts of produce and livestock. 'Generations after slavery has gone, the lowly status of these slave ancestors still matters.' He points out too that 'there are still slave descendants who work in the household of prosperous Ashanti without remuneration.'

Appiah points to a crucial feature of global enslavement now, and of slavery in Greek and Roman antiquity, and it is this that will lead to my focus on ancient Greece, a crucial site of the heritage of Western civilization:

Because people almost always think of slaves as belonging to a kind – a race, a tribe, a class, a family – that is suited to enslavement, the slave status tends to survive the abandonment of the formal institutions of slavery. (17)

And furthermore, even though legally slavery has been abolished, the condition of bondage can persist. This notion that slaves belong to a 'kind' that is suited to slavery, or that deserves slavery, or that benefits from slavery, provides the ideological underpinnings of slavery, and of the persistence of bondage into the present. Ira Berlin, in his study of the beginnings of racialised slavery in North America, *Many Thousands Gone*, discusses this question of difference:

Since slavery became exclusively identified with people of African descent in the New World, the slaveholders' explanation of their own domination generally took the form of racial ideologies. But African descent and the racialist pigmocracy that accompanied it was only one manifestation of the slaves' subordination. Even in societies where slave owner and slave admittedly shared the same origins, masters construed domination in 'racial' terms. Russian serf masters mused that the bones of their serfs were black.[24]

'Race,' and colour, visible or not, play a part in ideologies of enslavement.

The reasons given for enslaving others – for the simple economic drive for profit, for a sense of superiority, all the economic and social and emotional reasons for which people desire to dominate others, for whatever deeper reasons, having to do with an essential human aggression and need for domination, or with innate drives that are formed socially and culturally in specific ways by the world into which children grow – these seem to be culturally specific, particular to different cultures, different civilizations. The ancient Greeks had their story about barbarians, which passed through Aristotle into the racialised slavery of early modernity. But the Aryans of Vedic culture had their own story, specific to their culture and tradition, which still has consequences in present day slavery in South Asia. One of the hymns of the ancient Sanskrit text, the *Rig Veda*, describes the primal sacrifice, through which class stratification was attributed to the gods:

'When they divided Purusha, in how many different portions did they arrange him? What became of his mouth, what of his two arms? What were his two thighs and his two feet called?

His mouth became the brahman; his two arms were made into the rajanya (kshatriya), his two thighs the vaishyas; from his two feet the shudra was born,'

The ancient text justifies the ideology of class (*varna*) difference, and produces the so-called caste system, so misnamed by the Portugese, that still haunts the polity of India. Stanley Wolpert discusses this feature of early Indian civilization:

The *shudras*, who did the menial labour, may originally have been pre-Aryan *dasas*, reduced to serfdom or slavery by captivity and easily kept in lowly status because of darker skin colour. The Sanskrit word that came to mean 'class' (*varna*) and that is still used with the modifiers *brahman, kshatriya, vaishya*, and *shudra* to identify the four broadest categories of Hindu caste society, originally meant 'covering,' associated with skin covering and its varying colours. Each *varna* had its distinguishing colour; white for *brahmans*, red for *kshatriyas*, brown for *vaishyas*, and black for *shudras*. Acute colour consciousness thus developed early during India's Aryan age and has since remained a significant factor in reinforcing the hierarchical social attitudes that are so deeply embedded in Indian civilization. There is no reference to 'untouchables' in the Rig Veda, but fears of pollution became so pervasive in Indian society that it is difficult to believe they were not, in fact, pre-Aryan in origin. . . .

While all *shudras* were . . . held to be fully a life below the three higher 'twice-born' classes . . . some were considered so much less worthy than others that they were cast beyond the pale of recognized society.[25]

Although the myth of the Purusha, the cosmic man and his sacrifice, does not identify specifically those who will be enslaved, it points to the darker-skinned indigenous people who are banished to the lowest level of the social hierarchy, and may still be deployed, consciously or as an element of a political unconscious, as a justification for the enslavement of workers in the present. James C. Scott, in *Domination and the Arts of Resistance*, points to the resistance of the so-called 'scheduled castes and tribes' to the ideology inherited from the Vedic text:

Among untouchables in India there is persuasive evidence that the Hindu doctrines that would legitimize caste-domination are negated, reinterpreted, or ignored. Scheduled castes are much less likely than Brahmins to believe that the doctrine of karma explains their present condition . . .[26]

There have been conversions of such groups from Hinduism to Buddhism, Christianity, and Islam.

My point is that there are many explanations for the cruelty of human beings toward one another. Some theorists argue that the drive to own, dominate, use and subjugate other human beings may be innate in our species, and they point to other animals that they see as ruthless and bloody in tooth or claw. Others identify torture and slavery as features of pre-enlightenment, of pre-enlightened societies of the past, although the twentieth century, and what we have seen so far of the twenty-first, must lead us to reconsider whether such practices are behind us. Slavery might be an element of social and economic relationships typical of forms of production that encourage conflict and struggle, a vestige of an 'ancient' or even a 'slave mode of production.' Someone of a psychoanalytic bent might see the drive to dominate, own or enslave as a transhistorical feature of psyches damaged over millennia by cruelties of childhood. In any case, those civilizations that engaged in slavery developed myths, theories, ideologies, often based on the classical religions, that allowed some persons to dominate others, or even insisted that others be dominated, and these ideas generated in the classical phases of such civilizations have a persistence and a potency that cannot be underestimated. Just as most cultures in the historical period have discriminated against women, developed ideologies to justify their subjection and subjugation, control of their movements and sexual lives, ideologies that differ widely, so the ideologies of domination of slaves vary as well. Some societies imagine women to be so innately lustful that they must be locked up, others see them as so fragile and innocent that they must be cloistered. These are familiar stories, and they have their counterparts in the worldwide practice of slavery. Although there may be a convergence of such narratives at present, or a consensus on the part of slave-holders and slave-traffickers, that in general some inhabitants of failed states, especially in the global South, are natural slaves, in the past the specific justifications for slavery have varied widely, and this book is about one of those varieties, that of Western civilization and of the Greek beginnings of such a narrative in the West, that branch descended from Athens rather than Jerusalem, though of course Jerusalem had its slaves as well, and its own story about why such persons should be slaves.

In the next chapter, I will move from the slaves of today to the early modern and modern institution of racialised slavery, in which Africans brought to the New World, replacing indentured servants and enslaved indigenous peoples, became the preferred targets of slavery in the context of early capitalism.

CHAPTER II

RACIALISED SLAVERY

I was born May 1815, of a slave mother, in Shelby County, Kentucky, and was claimed as the property of David White Esq. He came into the possession of my mother long before I was born. I was brought up in the Counties of Shelby, Henry, Oldham, and Trimble. Or, more correctly speaking, in the above counties, I may safely say, I was flogged up; for where I should have received moral, mental, and religious instruction, I received stripes without number, the object of which was to degrade and keep me in subordination.

Henry Bibb, *Narrative of the Life of Henry Bibb*

If I began this book's first chapter with the voices of living slaves, it is because it is so easy to forget the human suffering of slaves now dead, especially those as far in the past as the ancient world of Greek and Roman classical civilization. In this chapter I will discuss the more recent past, the racialised slavery of European and American modernity, including North and South America, site of the greatest concentration of slavery since the *latifundia*, the agricultural slave factories of the ancient Romans.[1] Such slavery can itself be seen objectively, as a distant feature of a remote past, but it is nonetheless more accessible than that of the ancient world, in part because we do have evidence that corresponds more fully with our post-modern, individual sense of experience. In other words, we have both novels, and slave narratives, the words of slaves themselves, that open up the life-worlds of the racialised slaves of early modernity, and that will lead me eventually, in later chapters, into the world of Greek antiquity. In this chapter I will discuss not only such evidence, but also the work of historians and political theorists who have traced the history of this period.

Of course there are problems with assuming that the individual psyches, the persons of our own historical period, products of enlightenment, of subjectification of a modern sort, individuals affected at least marginally by psychoanalytic ideas of selfhood, are identical to those of more remote periods of history. Modern and postmodern selves are marked by their historical time – and all the associations of private property and the self as private property, the inner life of the conscious or unconscious mind – all of these are ways of understanding experience very different, as far as we can tell, from those of many people in other cultures distant temporally or even simply geographically from our own. Slave narratives of the present can let us share to some degree the experiences of persons more like us, who have suffered from enslavement, although there are limits, even there, to the capacity of any single person to share the experience of another. But to know the experience of someone now long dead, through his or her own testimony, or even more remotely through representation by another, a master, for example, involves great obstacles. If an ancient slave never wrote an autobiography, we are shut off from the trajectory of a slave's life, his or her career, but it is also a significant fact about how people understood their lives in antiquity. There were no autobiographies until late in antiquity; no single individual saw the point of telling the story of his or her own life.[2] This means not that ancient people just forgot to record the events of their lives, or that they couldn't be bothered, but that shaping a narrative in terms of a passage from one's own birth to life's end was not a meaningful act. And the psychological probing, the musings, the recollections and inner life that modern individuals record, may not have been features of the psychic life of ancient persons. So a novel like Toni Morrison's *Beloved*, for example, which leads readers into the psychic worlds of her characters, records events and experiences as imagined by someone inhabiting our world. The slave narratives we have from the nineteenth century in America are documents of the nineteenth century, untouched by the stylistic innovations of modernism, magic realism and postmodernism, and they therefore have the matter-of-fact, discursive quality of many other texts of their period. And narratives by non-slaves, about slaves, depict mastery or sometimes, self-interested and self-soothing empathy that masks other impulses.[3] In this chapter I focus more on the accounts of slavery in North America than elsewhere, than in Latin America, Brazil and the Caribbean, only because they are more familiar to me, just as the slaves of Greek antiquity are more familiar because I am a Hellenist. But we must remember always that racialised slavery occurred not just in the colonies that eventually became the United States of America, then fell apart in the Civil War, the War Between the States, as it is sometimes called, only to be reunited afterwards. Racialised slavery and its aftermaths had great impact also on all the states of the Americas, French, Dutch, Spanish, Portugese colonies, an impact still felt throughout what was once called the New World. And that has its effects also on British and European societies of the present, as the citizens of once-colonised overseas possessions, members of commonwealths and empires, come to the metropolis, and participate in the life of those colonising sites of empire. These populations, the people of Martinique and Haiti, of Barbados and Jamaica and other locations in the new world, have changed the social worlds of once homogeneous British and European states forever.

Sherley Anne Williams' *Dessa Rose*

Rather than analyzing Toni Morrison's brilliant novel *Beloved*, widely read and commented on, I want to turn first to another twentieth-century novel that concerns American slavery, Sherley Anne Williams's *Dessa Rose*, as a transition to the narratives written by slaves themselves in the eighteenth and nineteenth centuries. One of its most striking aspects of this novel is its psychological depth in a plurality of voices, rendered not in a mosaic, or a blended narrative of recollection and direct speech, but rather in distinct sections that call attention to the varied rhetorics of discourses of the nineteenth century. In the novel, the writer Adam Nehemiah, author of one book, *The Masters' Complete Guide to Dealing with Slaves and Other Dependents*, is composing a second such volume to be called *The Roots of Rebellion in the Slave Population and Some Means of Eradicating Them*. He interviews the slave he calls Odessa, who led a slave revolt, escaping from a coffle, a train of slaves to be sold, after she attacked her owners for killing her lover, Kaine. The novel gives the reader the voice of Nehemiah, the social-climbing writer who strives to rise above his station and become one of the planter class, but must make his way for now by writing. He says of his interviews with 'Dessa,' 'It is obvious that I must speak with her again, perhaps several more times; she answers questions in a random manner, a loquacious, roundabout fashion – if, indeed, she can be brought to answer them at all. This, to one of my habits, is exasperating to the point of fury.'[4] Williams also gives us the voice of Dessa, in dialect, and she sings in her isolation, fettered and pregnant and waiting for execution:

> Lawd, give me wings like Noah's dove
> Lawd, give me wings like Noah's dove
> I'd fly cross the fields to the one I love
> Say, hello, darling; say how you be (36)

Themes from the Hebrew Bible, with its narratives of flight and liberation from slavery, to be discussed in chapter three, catch the imagination of this woman, even though 'Masa say he don't be liking religion in his slaves.' (37)

Dessa is rescued from captivity and her interrogation by Nehemiah, with the help of some of those from the coffle who had escaped, and they try to find a maroon community, a group of fugitive slaves living together in the wilderness. She ends up, with her baby, in the house of a white woman, also recently having given birth; the African Americans of the household are not her slaves, but runaways whom she keeps with her to help her with her house and farm, since her husband has deserted her. And these people forge a community of their own; the white woman nurses the black baby, and the women share a lover. Then the black people make a plan; in Dessa's voice:

> They started talking about West. They didn't none of them know that much about it, but Harker talked about it like he'd seen the forests and the streams, the river where slavery couldn't cross over cause everybody on that side was free. (171)

They all decide to go west together, financing their journey by selling themselves and then running away, on to the next town to be sold again, with the white mistress providing a cover for them.

When Nehemiah has finally hunted down Dessa Rose, he recognizes her but tries to prove she is the runaway he is hunting through the markings on her body; the wanted poster offers a hundred-dollar reward to a woman 'branded, eh, sheriff, R on the thigh, whipscarred about the hips.' (222) The black women and the white together defy the slave-hunter, who reveals himself as obsessed with Odessa, claiming that he relies on 'Science. Research. The mind of the darky.' (232) The women, black and white, runaway slave and free, walk out of the jail together.

In this twentieth-century novel, Williams uses slave narratives, records and the work of Angela Davis and Herbert Aptheker to create a powerful narrative of slowly, painfully forged solidarity among women, in a way that not only speaks to the feminism of the 1980s, the racial divide within the feminist movement of the late twentieth century, but also to the suffering and resilience of the African-American community of the nineteenth century, and the hope of a common purpose and struggle engaged in by black and white.

The Life of Olaudah Equiano, or Gustavus Vassa, the African, Written by Himself

The slaves and free persons of Dessa Rose are fictional characters, imagined into existence by their twentieth-century creator. Not a novel, the slave narrative that draws readers closest to the early experience of a captured slave is that of Olaudah Equiano, published in London in 1789. His is a rich and vivid account of travel from Africa to the Americas, and affords rich detail concerning the way of life of all he met in his journeys, forced and later, when he was a free man. His story begins in Benin, in the part of Africa he calls 'Guinea,' in which, he writes 'the trade for slaves is carried on.'⁵ His father was an elder, a chief, and was marked with a cut across the top of his forehead, making a scar like the one the author himself was destined to receive. His father was a judge and had imposed punishments making it clear that slavery existed in this society, used in cases of adultery, for example. (6) Equiano goes on to describe in ethnographic detail the everyday life of the people he was soon to leave behind, noting that they took prisoners of war, and kidnapped others, who were then enslaved, 'perhaps . . . incited to this by those traders who brought . . . European goods . . .' (11):

> When a trader wants slaves, he applies to a chief for them, and tempts him with his wares. It is not extraordinary, if on this occasion he yields to the temptation with as little firmness, and accepts the price of his fellow creature's liberty, with as little reluctance as the enlightened merchant. (11)

The chief 'falls on his neighbours,' enslaves them if he wins, and is killed with no possibility of ransom if he loses the battle. Yet Equiano describes the condition of these slaves as less terrible than that of the slaves in the West Indies, which he will come to later in his story; in Africa itself, the slaves 'do no more work than other members of the community, even their master; their food, clothing and lodging were nearly the same . . . Some of these slaves even have slaves under them as their own property, and for their own use.' (12) Equiano's father himself had many slaves. (19)

After this autobiographical and ethnographical account, Equiano goes on to describe his 'day of slavery,' as the ancient Greeks would call it, the day in which his freedom was lost to him.

One day when all our people were gone out to their works as usual, and only I and my dear sister were left to mind the house, two men and a woman got over our walls, and in a moment seized us both, and, without giving us time to cry out, or to make resistance, they stopped our mouths, and ran off with us into the nearest wood. (20)

Equiano himself is carried in a sack, and he and his sister comfort each other for a night, weeping, until the two are separated. The boy becomes a slave in the household of another chieftain, in a family that speaks his own language. He tries to escape, is sold again, encounters his sister and is allowed to hold her hands all night, before they are separated again, this time for good. Equiano is sold again, for 'one hundred and seventy-two' little white shells. He is passed along until he reaches the coast and is forced aboard a slave ship.

When I looked round the ship too, and saw a large furnace of copper boiling, and a multitude of black people of every description chained together, every one of their countenances expressing dejection and sorrow, I no longer doubted of my fate; and, quite overpowered with horror and anguished, I fell motionless on the deck and fainted. (27)

Equiano fears he will be eaten by the white men on the ship. And he describes the hideous conditions of the slave ship – the stench, 'absolutely pestilential,' 'the galling of the chains,' 'the filth of the necessary tubs, into which the children often fell, and were almost suffocated, the shrieks of the women, and the groans of the dying' (30)[6] Finally, after weeks of suffering, witnessing two slaves chained together jumping through the netting around the ship into the sea, watching suicide, deaths, flogging and suffocation, Equiano reaches land at last and the slaves are told by other slaves that they are not to be eaten, but to work. (32) The passengers are sold, friends and relatives separated and he begins life in the New World.

Equiano has many adventures, traveling from the West Indies to Virginia, to England and Germany, is entangled in war, returns to the West Indies, where he is sold again and spends the years 1763 to 1766. He sees slaves branded, hung with chains, and describes instruments of torture – iron muzzle, thumb-screws – and beatings. He himself is beaten and mangled in Georgia. Finally he manages to gain enough money to purchase his freedom and buys manumission. He converts to Christianity and eventually becomes a crusader against slavery, joining in a petition to the queen:

> I presume, therefore, gracious Queen, to implore your interposition with your royal consort, in favour of the wretched Africans; that, by your Majesty's benevolent influence, a period may now be put to their misery – and that they may be raised from the condition of brutes, to which they are at present degraded, to the rights and situation of freemen, and admitted to partake of the blessings of your Majesty's happy government ... (188)

The petition is signed 'Gustavus Vassa, The Oppressed Ethiopian.'[7]

Doubts have been raised concerning the authenticity of Equiano's autobiography, especially in relation to his ethnographic accounts of life in Africa. A notice of baptism, found in Westminster, in England, records him, on 9 February 1759, as 'Gustavus Vassa a Black born in Carolina 12 years old.' Some argue that the details of his childhood in Africa may be based on reading other's accounts, rather than on childhood experience. Nonetheless, this earliest slave narrative bears testimony not only to practices of enslavement within Africa, of Africans by Africans, but also to the commodity trade in slaves in eighteenth-century capitalist networks of exchange, where slaves were traded by Africans to Europeans, who carried them in terrible conditions through the 'middle passage,' to be exchanged for raw materials that were then brought back to Europe.

The History of Racialised Slavery

The international slave trade to which Olaudah Equiano fell victim had a long and painful history. In fact, slavery had never vanished from the

Mediterranean and European world in the wake of the fall of the Roman Empire. As will become clear in the chapters that follow, the Greeks and the Romans had not practiced enslavement of human beings based on their so-called 'racial' nature, features of the body such as skin colour or hair.

Some of the slaves, some of the poor of the latter Roman Empire, especially in the West, became *coloni*, that is, serfs tied to the land, although slavery itself persisted as an institution through the medieval period. As the complex social, economic and political organization of the Roman imperial system fell into disarray, collapsing from within and besieged by outsiders, some people became attached to the land and subordinate to lords, without their status coinciding precisely with that of the slaves of the former Roman Empire. As Christianity began to provide an alternative structure of bishoprics and ecclesiastic courts to supplant those of the Roman state, canon law replaced to some degree the legal system of the Romans, which had codified the status of slaves and the rights of their masters, formally addressing questions of manumission and other details, in the code of Justinian. Throughout the medieval period, however, there continued to be slaves in a legal sense, persons subject to their masters' coercion and violence, to social death and to dishonour. Robin Blackburn cites the Domesday Book of 1086, in which 'slaves were still reported to comprise as much as one-tenth of England's population, with the figure rising to a fifth in the West Country. From this point on, evidence for true slaves in England declines sharply.'[7] There were declining numbers in South Western Europe also. The English word 'slave' is derived from 'Slav', that is, a Slavic person. The Vikings and Italian slave-traders enslaved Slavs in great numbers between the tenth and the sixteenth centuries, and their name came to stand for the generic type, including Muslims who were enslaved in large numbers on the Iberian peninsula and elsewhere.

With the coming of the third great Abrahamic monotheism, Islam, slavery changed in many ways. Christians were allowed to enslave and own Muslim slaves so long as they remained Muslim, and vice versa. And there are many instances of 'Moorish' slaves in late medieval and early Renaissance Europe. Some of these were black Africans. And, gradually, as David Brion

Davis recounts in his seminal book, *The Problem of Slavery in Western Culture*, slavery came to linked with these Africans, who were assimilated to the Old Testament sons of Ham, and seen to be worthy of enslavement by white Europeans and, eventually, by the white colonists of the New World.[8]

It is these black Africans who were loaded on to the ships of English, Dutch and Portugese slave-traders, and carried across the Atlantic in what was called the 'middle passage.' In his study of the slave ship, Marcus Rediker confirms the testimony of Olaudah Equiano in greatest detail, but is also filled with admiration at the creativity of those who survived these terrible journeys:

> Over the almost four hundred years of the slave trade, from the late fifteenth to the late nineteenth century, 12.4 million souls were loaded onto slave ships and carried through a 'Middle Passage' across the Atlantic to hundreds of delivery points stretched over thousands of miles. Along the dreadful way, 1.8 million of them died, their bodies cast overboard to the sharks that followed the ships. Most of the 10.6 million who survived were thrown into the bloody maw of a killing plantation system, which they would in turn resist in all ways imaginable.[9]

He notes the 'drama' that 'grew from conflict and cooperation among the enslaved themselves as people of different classes, ethnicities and genders were thrown together down in the horror-filled lower deck of the slave ship.' (7) Against all odds, people in these hideous conditions 'fashioned new languages, new cultural practices, new bonds and a nascent community . . .' (8) Rediker emphasizes the constant terror experienced by those enslaved and transported in the ghastly ships of the slave trade, yet also finds good deeds, 'enslaved people caring for diseased and dying seamen in Caribbean ports.' (355) The enslaved found ways of resisting the hellish circumstances in which they found themselves, defying the dehumanization of ship-captains, some sailors and traders, in ways that pointed forward to forms of overt and covert resistance on the plantations of the new world.

The theoretical, rhetorical justifications for racialised slavery will be discussed in the next chapter. Here I want to recount the historical changes that produced a vast system of enslavement of kidnapped, captured and traded Africans in the New World, in North America, in the Caribbean and in South America. Olaudah Equiano stands near the beginnings of the process, and Frederick Douglass survives its end, although, as some scholars have argued, slavery persists in the New World under a different name.[10]

Robin Blackburn, in a two-volume study, presents the history of the beginnings of racialised slavery in the West, and its overthrow.[11] He shows how deeply imbricated were capitalism and slavery in its new forms, and argues that 'profits from slavery . . . helped to furnish some of the conditions for a global industrial monopoly.' (6) This, then, is a very different context for slavery from that of ancient Greece and Rome, operating in a disembedded fashion, that is, torn away from its traditional contexts, and in this modern version of slavery we encounter new forms of the state, and of the nation-state, but also rationalization of the slave system, the work of the market, new administrative bureaucracies and 'an individualist sensibility.' (4) All these add up to a very different slave system from that of antiquity.

Rather than seeing slavery as a vestige from the past, a remnant of older practices, of tradition and backwardness, Blackburn sees the slavery of modernity as an economic, social and political form taking advantage of the great flexibility of slavery as a transhistorical institution. The most marked difference is the use of racial difference in identity to mark those born to be free, those born to be slaves:

> The New World slave was caught up in systems of social identification and surveillance which marked him as a black, and closely regulated his every action. (5)

In the new economic circumstances of the period, the question of so-called 'race' assumed growing importance:

In the racial theory, which became peculiarly associated with plantation slavery, the abstracted physiological characters of skin colour and phenotype came to be seen as the decisive criteria of race, a term which had hitherto had more a sense of family or kind, nature or culture. (15)

As Blackburn notes, not all black persons were slaves, but most were; whites were assumed to be free, blacks slaves. Free and freed blacks were always at risk of being re-enslaved if they were unable to prove their status. And, as Saidiya Hartman makes clear in *Scenes of Subjection: Terror, Slavery, and Self-Making in Nineteenth-Century America*, '... there was no relation to blackness outside the terms of this use of, entitlement to, and occupation of the captive body, for even the status of free blacks was shaped and compromised by the existence of slavery.'[12]

Slavery had become a marginal feature of European societies until the period of exploration and discovery that began in the fifteenth century CE. The encounter with indigenous peoples shocked the voyagers, and one of their responses was to find these people enslavable. As their economies changed, and the indigenous peoples of the new world failed to meet their expectations as labourers and breeders of new labourers, they began to see the continent of Africa, somewhat familiar in antiquity and the middle ages, as the source of new bodies to perform the work of building the new world. In the rivalry of the various early modern European states, including Britain, Spain and the Netherlands, Portugal and France, the willingness to enslave and to trade slaves provided an economic opportunity that was seized upon by all. Slavery had survived in theory, if not in practice, from the time of the Romans, and it was redeployed in the new circumstances of colonialism.

The Portugese began the slave trade with Africa, beginning with their voyages of discovery in the fifteenth century, sponsored at first by the son of Joao I, Prince Henry 'the Navigator.' The Portugese began by seeking gold, reaching the 'Gold Coast' in 1470; Vasco da Gama set out in 1497 and sailed around the Cape of Good Hope, all the way to India, in a journey recollected in the great epic poem of Camoes, the *Lusiads*, published in 1572, which depicts the encounter of the sailors with a black community:

> I saw a stranger with a black skin
> They had captured, making his sweet harvest
> Of honey from the wild bees in the forest.
>
> He looked thunderstruck, like a man
> Never placed in such an extreme;
> He could not understand us, nor we him
> Who seemed wilder than Polyphemus. (5.27–8)[13]

The poet cannot express the strangeness of the encounter with the black man except to compare it to the captivity of the Homeric hero Odysseus, in the cave of the Cyclops. The next day the 'fellows' of this first black man, 'naked, and blacker than seemed possible' (30), appear and seem to want more of the trinkets offered to their friend – beads, bells and rattles, a bonnet. One of the sailors tries to explore further into the community, but 'a bold Ethiopian' and 'a battalion of blacks' ambush the Portugese, who 'returned so super-added a reply/ It was not just those bonnets that they wear/Were crimson at the end of this affair!' (33) And the adventurers sail on.

But before Vasco da Gama's expedition of 1497, based in part on the gold obtained through trading with Africa, the Portugese had discovered the great profit to be gained from trading slaves:

> In 1441 a Portugese expedition on the West African coast captured two nobles; some gold was acquired by handing them back .... In 1444 a cargo of 235 captives comprising both 'whites' (Berbers) and 'blacks,' were seized in another Portugese raid on the African coast, and taken for division and disposal to Lagos in the Algarve. However, the Portugese captains soon discovered that they could, with less trouble and expense, also buy slaves and sell them to those involved in settling the islands ... (Blackburn, 102)

Other Africans, like those described by Olaudah Equiano and Kwame Anthony Appiah, slaveholders themselves of large numbers of war captives, sold slaves to merchants who then sold them on to the Portugese traders. This commerce eventually received a papal blessing, on the grounds of its Christianizing the islands of Madeira and the Azores, as well as the slaves themselves. The captives were initially taken to Lisbon and sold to Portugese or Spaniards, or taken to the islands. But eventually the trade reached beyond Europe, into the Atlantic, across the Atlantic. Blackburn details how, after about 1520, the Portugese began selling increasing numbers of slaves destined for Latin America, sold first to traders in Seville and then transported on to the Americas. The Spanish controlled more land, needed more slaves, and, as in other zones of the new continent, discovered problems in the enslavement of, and rendering productive and reproductive, the indigenous peoples. The Africans had initially been enslaved by their own people, or people close to them, they were heterogeneously jumbled together, often not speaking one another's languages, and they had skills appropriate to the needs of the colonies. The colonizers developed some religious qualms, finally, about conquering, converting and enslaving them, yet the Africans soon supplanted the native peoples as workers, enslaved and transported not only by the Portugese and the Spanish, but also by the Dutch. And the English joined in the enterprise. At first, English indentured servants provided the labour force on English plantations, but, eventually, the colonies of the English, begun in the seventeenth century, relied, in the Caribbean, on Barbados and Jamaica, in the smaller settlements on other islands, and in North America, on slave labourers. Blackburn reminds us that the luxuries of neo-classical London depended on slavery in the colonies; the wealthy consumed tobacco, sugar, coffee, tea and chocolate, and the coffee houses needed their imports to survive and flourish. These commodities could not be produced in England itself.

Slaves in America

The history of slavery in North America stretches from the earliest slave ventures in the English colonies, until the Emancipation Proclamation of 1865. And its consequences endure into the present, as the racialisation of slavery, the uprooting of people from their native lands, the breaking up of families in Africa and families formed in America during the time that slavery was legal, have had enduring impact on the lives of African Americans throughout the history of the colonies and of the United States.

Slavery in all the Americas benefited the farmers who were exporting their goods to Europe and to American cities. At first, slaves in Latin America were imported to engage in mining, as the indigenous peoples died at alarming rates due to the importation of diseases from Europe. The imported African slaves were soon turned to cultivation of coffee and sugar; sugar became the most important industry on the Caribbean Islands, and the plantation owners who profited from the labour often returned to England, leaving behind overseers who worked the labourers ruthlessly. It was believed that sugar was best cultivated by slaves, and more and more were traded to supply the sugar mills of the triangular trade of slaves, sugar and rum. The first slaves in North America arrived in 1619, and, as indentured servants were replaced by slaves, the numbers of arrivals grew. Indentured workers, white English persons or Europeans, often served for terms as short as three years and were less satisfactory for plantation work, and the supply of such indentured servants declined as economic conditions improved in England. The first crop tended by slaves in Virginia was tobacco, but the great concentration of slaves came with the invention of the cotton gin by Eli Whitney in 1793.

The founders of the United States of America, at their constitutional convention of 1787, debated the importation of slaves. George Mason declared that slavery was immoral and dangerous; Charles Pinckney replied: "'If slavery be wrong, it is justified by the example of all the world. He cited the case of Greece, Rome and other ancient States,"' as James Madison reports.[14] Thomas Jefferson also participated in the discussion, arguing vigorously for black inferiority, and claiming that the few Roman slaves who had been great artists, like Epictetus and Terence, both freed slaves, 'were of the race of whites.' (96) (This is an assertion impossible to prove of Terence, for example, who was African, like the sainted Augustine.) The cultivation of cotton skyrocketed, and dominated the economies of the new states of Alabama, Mississippi, Texas and Louisiana. Cotton was grown on smaller plantations than was sugar and required less capital investment in slaves. At its height, the American plantation slave system dominated the Southern economy as African American slaves comprised almost forty percent of the population of the Southern states. Up to sixty-three percent of the inhabitants of South Carolina in 1720 were slaves and more than half the population in Mississippi in 1860. Ira Berlin delineates the sub-cultures of slavery within the larger context of the colonies that became the United States distinguishing 'four different slave societies: one in the North; another in the Chesapeake region; a third in the coastal lowcountry of South Carolina, Georgia and Florida; yet another in the lower Mississippi Valley.'[15] And he divides the history of slavery in the earlier centuries in North America into three distinct sets of experiences: 'that of the *charter generations*, defined as the first arrivals, their children and in some cases their grandchildren; the *plantation generations*, who were forced to grow the great staples; and the *revolutionary generations*, who grasped the promise of freedom and faced a resurgent slave regime.' (12) What followed was the nineteenth-century struggle between north and south, slave and free, that ended, in some sense, with the Emancipation Proclamation and the defeat of the southern, slave-owning states, in the Civil War.

Life on the plantations has been characterized by Achille Mbembe as one of the first instances of what Giorgio Agamben called the 'state of exception,' where 'the humanity of the slave appears as the perfect figure of a shadow.'[16] 'The slave is ... kept alive, but in a state of injury, in a phantom-like world of horrors and intense cruelty and profanity.' (21) Mbembe calls slave life 'a form of death-in-life.' And, as he further notes, crucial to the 'concatenation' of the terror formation that is slavery, is race. (22)[17] The culture of this world has been well-documented by scholars, although there are intense debates about such issues as the Christianization of the Africans enslaved and the degree to which it was possible for them to invent a new, hybrid society in the shadow of the owners and the constant threat of violence, death and sale.

Another slave narrative, *Incidents in the Life of a Slave Girl, Written by Herself*, by Harriet A. Jacobs, edited by L. Maria Child, offers a glimpse into the life of slaves in the nineteenth century before the so-called Civil War, or the War Between the States.[18] This account has had a somewhat complicated history, in that, when it was first published in 1861, it contained the name of the editor, a prominent abolitionist, but not the name of the author, who presented her life under the pseudonym of 'Linda Brent' in the text. But subsequent scholarship has uncovered the biography of the real Harriet Jacobs, 'who was born a slave in Edenton, North Carolina, around 1813.' (xv) Her family contained both free and slave relatives, including her grandmother, freed and living as a freedwoman in the same town; her father was the slave of a resident of the town, Andrew Knox, and 'probably the son of Knox's neighbour Henry Jacobs.' (xv) The author's mother was also a slave, whose master was the owner of a tavern in the town. Jacobs's parents both died when she was a child, and her mistress gave her in her will to a three-year-old child who lived near Jacobs's grandmother. The father of her mistress, called pseudonymously 'Dr. Flint' in the narrative, persecuted Jacobs as long as she lived in his vicinity, and, when she refused to submit to him, she was sent to a plantation. She tried to rescue her own children, who lived with her grandmother, from a similar fate, by running away, and sheltered herself for years in an attic in her grandmother's house. Her children were bought by their father, a white lawyer in the town; he had promised to free them, but never did so, and, after her escape to the north, Jacobs lived in constant fear that all would be recaptured and returned to the slave owners in North Carolina.

In addition to the sexual persecution to which Jacobs was constantly subjected by her master Dr. Flint, Jacobs's descriptions of life on the plantation reveal something of the everyday life of slaves in the antebellum south. In an episode remarkable for its sadism, but not seen as unique, Jacobs recounts one slavemaster's cruelty when a slave who attempted to escape continued whipping, was recaptured:

> This man considered punishment in his jail, on bread and water, after receiving hundreds of lashes, too mild for the poor slave's offence. Therefore he decided, after the overseer should have whipped him to his satisfaction, to have him placed between the screws of the cotton gin, to stay as long as he had been in the woods. (48)

The slave owner places the fugitive in this torture device, in a perversion of the instrument's use for the production of cotton, after he inflicts further beating, and then orders that he be washed with salt water, so that his flesh will not 'mortify.' (49) The slave is then screwed into the gin, with room only to turn to his side and back. 'When he had been in the press four days and five nights, the slave [who brought bread and water] informed his master . . . that a horrible stench came from the gin house. . . . When the press was unscrewed, the dead body was found partly eaten by rats and vermin.' (49)

Acts of resistance, of flight and defiance, persisted in the world of domination and sadism controlled by the slave owners. James C. Scott bases much of his important book, *Domination and the Arts of Resistance*, on reports of forms of struggle in the world of slaves and their masters, 'counter-conduct,' acts that defied the rules forbidding the slaves to learn to read and write, to consort with one another, to enjoy music, feasting and celebration, to have ordinary family life.[19] Scott points to the 'hidden transcripts,' things thought and said behind the masters' backs, acts that subverted the authoritarian hegemony of the slave owners. Scott recounts the words of a silent black cook whose daughter had been beaten by their master, and who expresses her anticipation of the day when she will 'see white folks shot down like de wolves when dey come hungry out o'de woods.' (5) She speaks these words in front of someone, a white governess from New

England, whom she trusts, or else she is so moved by anger that she cannot contain herself. Scott notes 'that the semi-clandestine culture of the slaves encouraged and celebrated theft from the masters and morally reproved any slave who would dare expose such a theft.' (188) Strategems of resistance, 'hidden transcripts,' included, as well as theft, 'pilfering, feigned ignorance, shirking or careless labour, footdragging, secret trade and production for sale, sabotage of crops, livestock and machinery, arson, flight and so on.' (188)

Harriet Jacobs reports that the news of the attempted rebellion by Nat Turner in 1831 reached her town. In Virginia, Turner had led his followers to revolt and they had killed fifty-five white persons, according to contemporary reports. As the editor Jean Yellin reports, 'Turner remained at large for more than nine weeks. Captured, tortured, jailed, interrogated and tried, he was executed on November 11. In the aftermath of the insurrection, a wave of white terror swept across the entire South.' (269)

Jacobs tells the story of how her town conducted an annual 'muster,' in which the whites dressed in military uniforms, and paraded with their muskets. On hearing of Turner's attempted rebellion, the town performed another such muster and searched all the houses, including that of Jacobs's freedwoman grandmother:

> It was a grand opportunity for the low whites, who had no negroes of their own to scourge. They exulted in such a chance to exercise a little brief authority, and show their subserviency to the slaveholders; not reflecting that the power which trampled on the coloured people also kept themselves in poverty, ignorance, and moral degradation. (64)

A mob captures 'a respected old coloured minister;' he had been found with some packets of shot in his house, used by his wife to balance her scales. The whites planned to shoot him on the court house green. After things calmed down, the slaves asked to be allowed once again to meet at their church out in the woods, which was surrounded by their cemetery.

'Their request was denied, and the church was demolished.' (67)

An entire chapter of Jacobs's narrative is devoted to the hypocrisy of the white Christian church with regard to slavery. Christianity was deemed a useful antidote to inclinations to rebellion and murder. A preacher sent by the slave owners commented on Ephesians 6.5: 'Servants, be obedient to them that are your masters according to the flesh, with fear and trembling, in singleness of your heart, as unto Christ.' (68) He also warned them against traditional practices surviving from the African past, 'tossing coffee-grounds with some wicked fortune teller, or cutting cards with another old hag':

> When your master's work is done, are you quietly together, thinking of the goodness of God to such sinful creatures? No, you are quarreling, and tying up little bags of roots to bury under the door-steps to poison each other with. (69)

The Christian religion of the masters urges obedience and acceptance of slavery, and tries to eradicate any traces of earlier rituals and religious cult carried with those stolen from Africa. The theology of Christianity in relation to slavery will be discussed in the next chapter, but this passage from Jacobs's memoir clarifies the degree to which Christianity supported the slave system in the south, even as the slaves themselves often turned it to their own purposes, reinscribing the exodus of the Hebrew slaves from Egypt, the freedom from bondage of the Babylonian captives in the Hebrew Bible, as inspiring narratives of liberation, and even as northern abolitionists appealed to Christian charity and the universality of Christianity's message in their resistance to slavery, which had never taken root so firmly in the smaller farms and in the cities of the northern states.

Jacobs was pursued sexually by her master, and she reflected on the ways in which the vulnerability of slave women to their owners affected all the relationships of the households that kept slaves:

> Southern women often marry a man knowing that he is the father of many little slaves. They do not trouble themselves about it. They

regard such children as property, as marketable as the pigs on the plantation; and it is seldom that they do not make them aware of this by passing them into the slavetrader's hands as soon as possible, and thus getting them out of their sight.

Families were destroyed, siblings separated, and all social relationships in this culture perverted and distorted by the facts of the commodification of human beings, the violence and coercion used to force them to work and the social death and dishonour that characterized this slave society.

Frederick Douglass

The autobiography of Frederick Douglass, a man once enslaved, who became an important figure in the American abolitionist movement, offers a glimpse of the experience of slavery from within, presented in retrospect as part of the campaign to eliminate slavery in the United States. As noted above, like other slave narratives, it does not have the familiar qualities of Morrison's or Williams' novels, *Dessa Rose* or *Beloved*, for example, writerly techniques of modernism, the stream-of-consciousness, access to the unconsciousness, temporal complexities, foreshadowing and flashbacks, all features that become part of the novel in the twentieth century, but it has a great rhetorical, testimonial power.

Douglass's autobiography was published in several versions. The first appeared as *The Narrative of the Life of Frederick Douglass* in 1845, soon after Douglass had escaped from enslavement, in 1838. *My Bondage and My Freedom*, a second autobiography, appeared in 1855, and another, final version, entitled *Life and Times of Frederick Douglass*, in 1881. The 'Narrative,' the earliest of these texts, appears with the curious subtitle, 'Written by Himself,' as if to emphasize that it was not penned by the man who wrote its preface, the noted Northern abolitionist William Lloyd Garrison, or some other abolitionist, since many slave narratives of the day were in fact written by abolitionists rather than the freed slaves whose names appeared on the books' covers. The white abolitionists' rhetoric often appears hortatory and dated, while Douglass's does not. Garrison, publisher of the *Liberator*, ends his preface: 'Reader! are you with the man-stealers in sympathy and purpose, or on the side of their down-trodden victims?'[20] Douglass himself begins simply: 'I was born in Tuckahoe, near Hillsborough, and about twelve miles from Easton, in Talbot county, Maryland.' (23)

The most powerful moment of Douglass's account of his experiences as a slave comes when, having been sold, he was sent out to be 'broken' by a certain Mr. Covey, 'a professor of religion – a pious soul – a member and a class-leader in the Methodist church. All of this added weight to his reputation as a "nigger-breaker."' (87–88) Covey succeeds, by means of whipping and working Douglass mercilessly, in breaking him. But, in a famous passage, Douglass, addressing his reader directly, describes a turn: 'You have seen how a man was made a slave; you shall see how a slave was made a man.' (97) He fights back. Armed with a root, as advised by a fellow slave, a root that he was to carry on his right side, he resists the whipping Covey intends for him:

> I resolved to fight; and, suiting my action to the resolution, I seized
> Covey hard by the throat; and as I did so, I rose. (103)

The two men fight for two hours and, while Covey claims to have beaten his slave, Douglass says 'he had drawn no blood from me, but I had from him.' 'This battle with Mr. Covey was the turning-point in my career as a slave. I rekindled the few expiring embers of freedom, and revived within me a sense of my own manhood.' (104) Eventually, after much travail, Douglass escapes to Massachusetts and becomes part of the anti-slavery movement.

In *The Black Atlantic: Modernity and Double Consciousness*, Paul Gilroy delineated the shaping presence and contribution of the African diaspora to a hybrid modernity. And he discussed the crucial passage in the work of Hegel concerning lordship and bondage, arguing that 'The time has come for the primal history of modernity to be reconstructed from the slaves' points of view. These emerge in the especially acute consciousness of both life and freedom which is nurtured by the slave's "mortal terror of his sovereign master" and the continuing "trial by death" which slavery becomes for the male slave.'[21] Gilroy, following on Orlando Patterson's reading of Hegel in *Slavery and Social Death* (97–101), calls for a rewriting of the history of modernity:

> I want to propose that we read a section of Douglass's narrative as an alternative to Hegel: a supplement if not exactly a trans-coding of his account of the struggle between lord and bondsman. (60)

Douglass expresses the other side of the famous antagonism of Hegel's lord against his bondsman; in Hegel's account, 'one solipsistic combatant in the elemental struggle prefers his conqueror's version of reality to death and submits. He becomes the slave while the other achieves mastery. Douglass's version is quite different. For him, the slave actively prefers the possibility of death to the continuing condition of inhumanity on which plantation slavery depends.' (63) Rather than having the master tell the story of the slave, Douglass tells his own story, and affords an insight not only into the crucial and forming presence of the African diaspora in Western modernity, but also into the silence enforced on the slave by the master's narratives, empathetic or not.

Legacies of Racialised Slavery

Scholars of the nineteenth, twentieth, and twenty-first centuries have studied the effects of racialised slavery on those societies that once contained large populations of black African slaves. Even after liberation, while slavery was still legal in many states, as Saidiya Hartman points out in *Scenes of Subjection*, the effects of slavery on the freed, and on the relations between free black persons and whites in the United States, were inevitably marked by the existence of slavery. She argues that 'attempts to assert absolutist distinctions between slavery and freedom are untenable.' (13):

In place of the grand narrative of freedom, with its decisive events and incontrovertible advances, I offer an account that focuses on the ambivalent legacy of emancipation and the undeniably truncated opportunities available to the freed. (12)

Hartman looks beyond the published slave narratives, including those produced by the Works Progress Administration of the post-Depression New Deal of the twentieth century, attempting to recover the experience of the once-enslaved, considering them to be 'public performances' of slavery, encompassing 'the slave of the auction block and those sharing their recollection decades later.' (12)

The legacy of racialised slavery persists into the present, in the United States and in those European countries whose colonies and postcolonies continue to admit the descendants of slaves back in the metropolis. In the United States, 'the conception of race engendered by slavery and abolished by the Thirteenth Amendment [which abolished slavery] made 'black' virtually synonymous with 'slave' and 'white' with 'free' and created a master race and a subject race.' (Hartman, 187) Even the election of a president who is truly 'African American,' son of a Kenyan and a Kansan, cannot erase this legacy. For Americans whose genealogies derive from those southern states which once had huge populations of slaves, this history has repercussions in the present.

In *Slaves in the Family*, Edward Ball recounts his experiences, shared by many and now detailed in historical studies of the families of such prominent Americans as Thomas Jefferson, who had slave children. Published in 1999, Ball's memoir recalls his ancestors, some of whom owned plantations in South Carolina and owned slaves.[22] Ball does extensive research, seeks out and meets his relatives, descendants black and white, whatever that might mean in such circumstances, of the owners of the Ball family plantations.

Between 1698 and 1865, the 167 years the family was in the slave business, close to four thousand black people were born into slavery to the Balls or bought by them. The crop they raised was rice, whose colour and standard gave it the name Carolina Gold. After the Civil War, some of Ball places stayed in business as sharecrop farms with paid black labour until about 1900, when the rice market finally failed in the face of competition from Louisiana and Asia. (7)

The continuity of exploitation of African Americans by white slave owners and former slave owners was typical of the economies of many southern states, after the defeat of the confederacy. 'Share-cropping' was the name often given to the form of labour done on the plantations that survived the war, but, in fact, those African Americans still tied to the lands of their former owners were still bound in a form of slavery. Although the legal status of slave had been abolished, the criteria of slavery delineated by Orlando Patterson, of persons subjected to violence and coercion, having suffered social death and dishonour, persisted in new forms of subjugation and enforced labour.

This sorry history is told in Douglas Blackmon's *Slavery by Another Name: The Re-Enslavement of Black Americans from the Civil War to World War II*.[23] He points to the many corporations, and institutions in the United States that exploited and profited from the bondage of African Americans forced to work in super-exploitative situations, long after the legal end of slavery at the end of the Civil War. His list includes mining companies, U. S. Steel, banks, the many industries that used convict and bound labour that, for example, created the bricks of the city of Atlanta. In the course of his research, the author, who grew up in the Mississippi Delta and is the Atlanta editor of the *Wall Street Journal*, uncovers the role his own ancestors played in slavery and forced labour. He argues that:

Only by acknowledging the full extent of slavery's grip on US society – its intimate connections to present-day wealth and power, the depth of its injury to millions of black Americans, the shocking near-ness in time of its true end – can we reconcile the paradoxes of current American life. (402)

Of course, many would dispute Blackmon's identification of World War II with the end of American 'slavery by another name.' He sees the enforcement of the century-old Slavery Kidnapping Act in 1942, in the arrest of a white farmer who had held Alfred Irving, a black man, in slavery, beating and disfiguring him to force him to work on his farm in Texas, and further strengthening of the federal criminal code in the late forties and fifties, as proof of the commitment of the state to ending slavery in the United States. Yet, in his *If He Hollers Let Him Go*, first published in 1945, the novelist Chester Himes, who records life in the war-time plants of Los Angeles of the 1940s, depicts the on-going racism of American culture. The population of prisons at present in the United States is disproportionately African American, with forced labour and bondage part of the everyday life of prisoners held throughout the United States in the criminal justice system. As Loic Wacquant writes in an essay in *The New Left Review*:

> Not one but several 'peculiar institutions' have successively operated to define, confine and control African-Americans in the history of the United States. The first is *chattel slavery* as the pivot of the plantation economy and inceptive matrix of racial division from the colonial era to the Civil War. The second is the *Jim Crow* system of legally enforced discrimination and segregation from cradle to grave. . . . America's third special device for containing the descendants of slaves in the Northern industrial metropolis is the *ghetto* . . . .[24]

Wacquant argues that the fourth and subsequent institution to confine and control African Americans is the fusion of the remnants of the ghetto with 'the *carceral apparatus* with which it has become joined.' (41) He identifies a genealogical link between mass imprisonment and slavery; the consequences of racialised slavery continue to haunt not only the postcolonies of Africa, the multiracial societies of South America and the Caribbean and the metropoleis of those European countries that once engaged in the slave trade and exploited and profited from slaves' labour, but also the class and racially troubled contemporary United States.

Racialised slavery endured in the twentieth century not only in the form of penal servitude in the prisons of North America, but also in the slave labour camps of the Nazis, who enslaved not only Communists, Roma people and homosexuals, but also Jews, whom they maligned as a racially distinct people. Their slave camps, and death camps, were the culmination of millennia of anti-Semitism, based to some extent on Christian condemnation of the Jews as responsible for the death of Jesus in the time of the Roman Empire, although the Nazis themselves, not Christians, inherited this anti-Semitism and turned it into a new form of tribal and ethnic racialization and persecution. And the white government of South Africa, with its practices of apartheid, produced virtual enslavement of the black inhabitants of Southern Africa. The twenty-first century has already been witness not only to an immense traffic in slaves, as detailed in Chapter One, but also of the perpetuation of racialised enslavement by old enemies with ancient rationalizations; some argue, for example, that the camps of the Palestinian refugees constitute virtual enslavement of the former citizens of Palestine by the Israelis, with 'racial' justifications going back to the Hebrew Bible providing a rationale. And the twenty-first century has just begun.

CHAPTER III

ANCIENT IDEOLOGIES

Among barbarians the female and the slave have the same rank; and
the cause of this is that barbarians have no class of natural rulers, but
with them the conjugal partnership is a partnership of female slave
and male slave. Hence the saying of the poets—"'Tis meet that
Greeks should rule barbarians,' – implying the barbarian and slave
are the same in nature.

Aristotle, Politics 1.1.5 (1252b)

The owners of serfs in Russia asserted that the bones of their serfs were
black. In this chapter, I will consider the ancient ideologies that the slave
owners of early modern societies used to justify their practice of slavery. I
will focus, as noted before, on the West, and especially on the New World
slavery of North America, for which a great deal of evidence on this question exists. Robin Blackburn argues that slavery in the modern period was
not vestigial, not traditional, not a left-over from a more primitive past, an
earlier mode of economic and social organization, but rather a new set of
practices that took advantage of the flexibility of slavery to process the raw
materials of the new world, to send profit back to the metropolis, and to
spur the growth of the rivalrous economies of the various European states
competing for hegemony and domination in a globalizing situation. Yet
the arguments for enslavement not just of indigenous people discovered in
the new world, but also those Africans kidnapped, captured, bought and

sold to mine, grow sugar and tobacco and cotton in the colonies, were often not new. The justifications for owning others, for controlling their lives on plantations, for subjecting them to violence and coercion, social death and dishonour, often went back centuries, to the earlier forms of slavery typical not only of ancient Greece and Rome, but also of ancient Israel.

Slavery in the Hebrew Bible

One of the great narratives of liberation from slavery comes in the Hebrew Bible, in the story of the Egyptian captivity and exodus from Egypt of the Israelite slaves, more important even than another narrative of escape from captivity at the time of the Babylonian exile, traced not just in a historical account, but also in psalms echoed in the reggae music of the Rastafarians, descendants of slaves brought to Jamaica, who consider themselves similarly in exile from Ethiopia: 'By the waters of Babylon, there we sat down, and then we wept, as we remembered Zion,' as Bob Marley and the Wailers sang it (Psalm 137)(and also as Giuseppe Verdi recalled in *Nabucco*, with the beautiful hymn, 'Va pensiero.') Even before the Israelites' time in Egypt, the story of Noah sets up a hierarchy used later to justify the racialised slavery of the Americas; Noah curses his child Ham, who 'saw his nakedness,' (Gen. 9. 22), and his son Canaan: 'Cursed be Canaan; lowest of slaves shall he be to his brothers.' (Genesis 9.25).[1] And the offspring of Abraham and his slave, Hagar the Egyptian, their son Ishmael, is the father of another nation, which becomes the nation of Islam. The difference in kinds of human beings that will rationalize slavery has begun.

The enslavement of the Israelites in Egypt, however, is the paradigmatic event, one that generates the founding myth of the nation of Israel. It occurs in Genesis, when Joseph 'bought all the land of Egypt for Pharaoh . . . As for the people, he made slaves of them from one end of Egypt to the other.' (*Genesis* 47. 20–21) The sufferings of these slaves, four centuries after the death of Joseph, are recounted in Exodus 1: 'they set taskmasters over them to oppress them with forced labour. . . . The Egyptians became ruthless in imposing tasks on the Israelites, and made their lives bitter with hard service . . .' (Ex 1. 11–14). Then the Pharaoh orders the killing of every male child born to the Hebrew women; Moses escapes, and leads his people to freedom, after the Hebrews' god sends ten plagues on the Egyptians.

Yet, though this enslavement is recalled with bitterness and mourning after the Israelites reach and conquer the promised land, they become the 'slaves' of their god; that is, they are redeemed, in some sense bought out of slavery by their god, who claims them then as his own. The word *'ebed*, 'slave,' is metaphorically extended to those who serve the lord: Moses, in Deuteronomy 34.5, is called 'the servant of the Lord,' as is David (Psalm 18.1), the text using the word used of slaves. And the Israelites enslave their own people as well as others. Exodus, Leviticus, and Deuteronomy lay out the ancient laws concerning slaves; In Leviticus 25, for example, the god tells Moses not to treat as slaves those of the community so impoverished that they sell themselves.

> 'For they are my servants, whom I brought out of the land of Egypt; they shall not be sold as slaves are sold . . . As for the male and female slaves whom you may have, it is from the nations around you that you may acquire male and female slaves. You may also acquire them from among the aliens residing with you, and from their families that are with you, who have been born in your land; and they may be your property. You may keep them as a possession for your children after you, for them to inherit as property. These you may treat as slaves, but as for your fellow Israelites, no one shall rule over the other with harshness.' (*Leviticus* 25. 39–46).

Ambiguities persist here, often massaged by translators and editors, since the word *'ebed* means both servant and slave. Yet the text is clear that members of the Israelite community are to be treated differently from those of alien nations.

In the Introduction to the Pentateuch in the *New Oxford Annotated Bible*, the editor uses the example of slavery in the text of the Torah to point out that it is derived from various sources:

Slave laws concerning Hebrew or Israelite slaves are found in the Torah in Ex[odus] 21. 1–6, Lev[iticus] 25.39–46, and Deut[eronomy] 15.12–18. These laws cannot be reconciled in a straightforward fashion since three different notions of slavery underlie them. Most significant is the way in which Exodus differentiates between the treatment of male and female slaves, whereas Deuteronomy insists that they should both be treated similarly. While Exodus and Deuteronomy agree that a slave who loves his master may opt to remain a slave 'for life' (Ex. 21.6) or 'forever' (Deut 15.17). Lev 25 insists that slavery does not really exist, since slaves must be treated as 'hired or bound labourers,' and they may only serve 'until the year of the jubilee' (v. 40).[2]

Nonetheless, slavery, metaphorical and literal, is part of Israelite society, as it was for all the other societies of the Ancient Near East. The Egyptians seem to have held few slaves, some prisoners of war and foreigners. But in Babylonia:

> The relative number of slaves . . . in the seventh through the fourth centuries BC is difficult to determine but was sufficiently large to be of both economic and social significance. They, like cattle, constituted movable property and seem to have been one of the most important attributes of wealth. Hundreds of slaves worked on the temple estates, and there appear to have been three to five slaves in the average well-to-do family. Large business houses had dozens and even hundreds of slaves.[3]

The keeping of slaves was taken for granted in the theocratic societies of the ancient near east, and the temples of the ruling priests and monarchs employed many. Some were tattooed and marked with signs of their possession by particular temples or divinities, and this marking may have distinguished permanent from temporary dependents of the temple. In his extensive work on slavery in Babylonia, Muhammad Dandamaev describes the sacred markings on some slaves, markings that figure in later accounts, in the Hellenistic period, of the slaves of Asia Minor:

> Temple slaves were branded or marked with the symbols of gods to distinguish their status. Slaves of the Eanna temple in Uruk were marked with a star . . ., the symbol of the goddess Ishtar. This same star was used as a brand or mark on temple livestock . . . The mark was apparently branded on the slave's wrist, or perhaps the back of the hand, with a scorching hot, iron instrument called sindu. . . . The brand or mark of slaves of the Ezida temple in Borsippa was the image of a spade and a scribe's reed stylus, representing, respectively, the emblems of the gods Marduk and Nabu.[4]

The sacred writings of the Israelites also accept and regulate slavery, establishing hierarchies of enslavement, differentiating between those inside and outside the religious community and providing precedents for those who later looked to these writings as holy writ. Metaphorical enslavement of the faithful to the god himself echoes the literal enslavement of other human beings in the Hebrew community.

Slavery in Ancient Greek Political Theory

The first ancient historian whose work we have is Herodotus, who wrote in the fifth century BCE. Although he is concerned with the history of the war between the Greeks and the Persians at the beginning of that century, his work has anthropological dimensions that cast light on the Greeks' ideas concerning slavery. He describes societies surrounding the Greeks', as he investigates the developments that led to the Persian Wars, the invasion of Greece by Persian emperors and their armies, and he reveals Greek notions concerning the 'barbarians,' that is, those who did not speak Greek, who rather said 'bar-bar-bar,' and were therefore another kind – worthy of interest, certainly, but not dwellers in the *polis*, the unit of civilization most valued by the citizens of Hellas.

Herodotus details the decidedly un-Greek ways of the Scythians and the Egyptians, before recounting the incidents of the Persian Wars. And his representation of the Persian emperors shows their desire for absolute mastery over their subjects, including Greeks resident in the colonies of Asia Minor, which had fallen into the hands of the Persians. One Pythius, a Lydian, contributed lavishly to the campaign of Xerxes, the second emperor to invade Greece, and asked Xerxes for the favour of sparing his eldest son from military service in Xerxes's expeditionary force. Xerxes was enraged by the request: 'How dare you mention a son of yours, when you are no more than my slave, and should follow in my train with your whole household, wife and all?' (7.39)[5] The emperor orders his men to slice the son in question in half, and to place one half on each side of the road, so that the army could file between the two. The emperor's subjects are his slaves, and he exhibits a barbarian cruelty.

Much has been written concerning the Greeks' attitudes toward the barbarians, as exemplified by Herodotus, Thucydides, the Athenian tragedians and others.[6] They express a fascination with the lives of others, in other civilizations surrounding theirs, but also often characterize these societies as conditioned by enslavement, the situation where there is one free man, the emperor, for example, and all others slaves. And this justifies the common Greek practice of enslaving their neighbours. They enslaved not only Greek neighbours, but also and especially these barbarians, captured in war, kidnapped and sold in slave markets, as will be discussed in the next chapter. The question of slavery is deeply implicated in this issue of the barbarians and the ideology of slavery; in particular the view of 'natural slavery' relies on a differentiation between the Greeks and these others.[7]

G.E.M. de Sainte-Croix, in his masterly work *The Class Struggle in the Ancient Greek World,* elaborates on the relationship between Platonic thought, the difference between the Greeks and the barbarians, and the ideology of slavery:

Plato, like the vast majority of his contemporaries, took it for granted that it was right and proper for Greeks to enslave 'barbarians,' whom he calls their 'natural enemies.' In the funeral oration which he puts into the mouth of Aspasia (a parody of the standard Athenian speech delivered on such an occasion), he makes her say that war against fellow-Greeks should be pursued 'until victory,' but against barbarians 'to the death' . . . (*Menex*.242d)

In a dialogue thought to be late in Plato's works, the *Laws*, a discussion between two characters, an Athenian and a Spartan, questions the proper treatment of slaves, and presents alternative methods of governing them, without calling into question the inevitable presence of slaves in everyday life. The Athenian has alluded to the 'puzzling' status of the helots, Greeks themselves enslaved by the Spartans, and similar mass enslavement of the Mariandynians in Heraclea and the group enslaved in Thessaly; he goes on:

> . . . we should all say that a man should have the best and most trusty slaves who are to be had. Why, slaves have often enough before now show themselves far better men in every way than brothers or sons; they have often been the preservation of their masters' persons, property and whole family. (776d)

After this positive representation of the benefit slaves provide to the families of the free, the Athenian presents the opposing point of view to the Spartan, Megillus:

> And equally common the rival theory that slaves are rotten at heart, and no man of sense should ever put any trust in the whole tribe of them. (776e)

He cites the passage in the *Odyssey* in which the noble swineherd Eumaios, confronted with Odysseus's old dog Argos, about to die on a dunghill, had said that half the virtue of a man is taken from him by Zeus, on the day that slavery takes him. (*Odyssey* 17. 322–3) The masterless slave, like the masterless dog, fares ill.

Plato's Athenian continues to explore the different attitudes toward their slaves available to masters: 'A man takes one or other side in the dispute for himself. Some distrust the whole class and make their servants threefold – nay, a hundredfold – slaves at heart by the scourge and the lash, as though they were dealing with so many wild beasts.' (777a) As the interlocutors continue their conversation, focused on the construction of a more perfect community, they conclude that slaves kept together should not be derived from the same stock, like the Messenians, always on the verge of revolt, nor should they speak the same language. And, secondly, the Athenian proposes that slaves should be treated properly and with consideration, 'for their own sake indeed, but still more for ours.' (777d) Slaves should be chastised, not spoiled 'by mere admonitions as we should use to free men.' (777e) Even in a community governed by the best of laws, the presence of slaves is taken for granted, and the only question is their proper treatment. And proper treatment is required not only because of the potential danger in slaves who are treated badly, but also because the soul of the master must not be sullied with cruelty in relation to his slaves.

Plato, throughout his many dialogues, represents the presence of slaves in the everyday life of the Greek citizen, and uses, metaphorically, the idea of slavery and enslavement to describe the proper relationship among the elements of the soul, in the state and in the cosmos.[8] In the *Republic*, for example, the argument against behaving badly rests on the analogy between slavery and domination.

'Fine things are those that subordinate the beastlike parts of our nature to the human – or better, perhaps, to the divine; shameful ones are those that enslave the gentle to the savage . . .'

'. . . can it profit anyone to acquire gold unjustly if, by doing so, he enslaves the best part of himself to the most vicious? If he got the gold by enslaving his son and daughter to savage and evil men, it wouldn't profit him, no matter how much gold he got. How, then, could he fail to be wretched if he pitilessly enslaves the most divine part of himself to the most godless and polluted one and accepts golden gifts in return . . . .' (Plato, *Republic* 9, 589c-e)[9]

The soul of the individual must contain reason that enslaves, or dominates, its appetites and its force; the polis must contain a ruling class that enslaves the least of its residents; the cosmos must be seen as containing a principle of reason, good, divinity, that rules and enslaves the rest of that cosmos, its material existence distant from the metaphysical site of the master form. The doctrine of 'natural slavery' is implicit, although unstated, in the thinking of Plato.

Benjamin Isaac, in a polemical discussion of the invention of racism in classical antiquity, sees the Greeks and Romans as practicing an environmental determinism, establishing:

an essential contrast between a sturdy but mentally inadequate Europe and a soft Asia, the latter enjoying a good climate, with a healthy and wealthy population, suffering, however, from deficient masculinity and an insufficient sense of individual and collective independence. Aristotle developed the theory further, adding two elements which made it a useful conceptual tool for imperialists. He held that the Greeks occupied the ideal environment between Europe and Asia and were therefore supremely capable of ruling others. Aristotle's second addition is the claim that the inhabitants of Asia were servile by nature, or natural slaves, and therefore suited to be subjects of the Greeks.[10]

The potential lying in these conceptualizations is realized in the practices of early modern and modern racialised slavery.

In his *Politics*, the crucial formulation of ancient ideas of natural slavery, Plato's great student Aristotle allows the poet Euripides to express his belief that barbarians are natural slaves: 'It is meet/ that Greeks rule barbarians, not barbarians Greeks.' (*Iphigeneia in Aulis*, 1400–1401). In Euripides's tragedy *Iphigeneia in Aulis* the young Iphigeneia, daughter of Clytemnestra and the general Agamemnon, leader of the Greeks in the expedition to Troy, is lured to Aulis by the promise of marriage to the hero Achilles. She learns that she is rather to be sacrificed to the goddess Artemis, in expiation for the accidental killing of a sacred deer. After resisting, she accepts her terrible fate, bringing out Hellenic patriotism, and the hope that her death will bring peace to the Greeks. 'Because of me, never more will/ Barbarians wrong and ravish Greek women, / Drag them from happiness and their homes/In Hellas. The penalty will be paid/Fully for the shame and seizure of Helen.' (1379–83)[11] The girl believes that she will be the saviour of Greece, and that she, like the soldiers, will give her life for her people. In noble words, that seem to bear a heavy weight of irony for Euripides, she accepts her sacrifice, echoing that refrain of difference between Greeks and barbarians:

> To Greece I give this body of mine.
> Slay it in sacrifice and conquer Troy.
> These things coming to pass, Mother, will be
> A remembrance for you. They will be
> My children, my marriage; through the years
> My good name and my glory. *It is*
> *A right thing that Greeks rule barbarians,*
> *Not barbarians Greeks.* (1398–1401; italics added)

The horror of the young girl persuading herself to death, accepting her father's deceit and opportunism, in the hope of ending war, in its first production in 405 BCE, just after the death of Euripides himself, very near the worst days of the Peloponnesian War, may have excited both admiration for the courage of the young woman, and despair that such sacrifice of the young by the old seemed never to have satisfied the bloodthirsty gods. Aristotle cites the words of Iphigeneia to support his argument that Greeks should own barbarians, that foreigners, those who speak languages other than Greek, are 'natural' slaves.

The argument in *Politics*, this seminal text for political philosophy, is notoriously discontinuous, repetitious, self-contradictory and frustrating in its lack of logical development; its somewhat rambling, disjointed shape may derive from its source as lecture notes, taken as the master of the philosophical school spoke to his students. Yet it has been enormously influential, not only in Greek and Roman antiquity, but through the middle ages, the Renaissance and in the period of discovery and colonization of Africa and the Americas, and provides the most enduring and explicit legacy of antiquity for the justification of modern slavery.

Aristotle argues for the natural hierarchy of ruler and ruled, in the household and the *polis*, the so-called 'city-state' of classical Greece. His principle is that 'one that can foresee with his mind is naturally ruler and naturally master, and one that can do these things [or can carry out labour] with his body is subject and naturally a slave.' (*Politics* 1252b) Aristotle offers another definition as well, one that has a long life, especially in Rome: he calls the slave a 'living tool,' and a 'possession with a soul' (1253b30). In any case, he argues that the basic unit of human society is the household, and that 'the household in its perfect form consists of slaves and freemen.' (1253b)

The whole of Aristotle's treatment of slavery in *Politics* is difficult to follow, sometimes almost self-contradicting, with *non sequiturs* and responses to others' arguments never expressed but implicit. There is evidence, in this text, of arguments against slavery, and against the concept of natural slavery. He says at 1253b20:

> others maintain that for one man to be another man's master is contrary to nature, because it is only convention that makes the one a slave and the other a freeman and there is no difference between them by nature, and that therefore it is unjust, for it is based on force.

This must be a sign of polemics and debate concerning this issue among philosophers of the fourth century BCE or earlier. We have little remaining of such debates, since the tradition has preserved and privileged the philosophical lineage derived from Socrates, through Plato, to Aristotle. The texts or oral teachings of others, the pre-Socratics, the sophists, the Cynics, the early Stoics, sometimes taking positions contrary to orthodoxy, were not so well conserved, and often it is necessary to reconstruct their arguments through symptomatic reactions to them, as here in the text of Aristotle. He does not answer this argument immediately in his exposition, but returns to justifications for the naturalness of slavery. One of them is remarkable for its circularity, and rests not on the ethnic qualification of barbarian difference, but on the particular status of the slave: 'one who is a human being belonging by nature not to himself but to another is by nature a slave. (1251a15). The problems with this definition are obvious; anyone who is in fact a slave is naturally a slave. What Aristotle seems to argue further is that there is always a ruling and a subject factor in every relationship, and so a human being who submits to enslavement is naturally subjectable, naturally subjected. He goes back to the arguments of Plato here, citing the ideal situation of the soul ruling the body, the intelligence the appetites, human beings the animals, man ruling woman. (1254b15) It is actually a benefit for those who are inferior by nature to be governed by their superior. 'These are by nature slaves, for whom to be governed by this kind of authority is advantageous.' (1254b) Here Aristotle develops further his notion of natural slavery, in a repetition of his earlier argument now supplemented by an argument concerning reason, or *logos*:

> He is by nature a slave who is capable of belonging to another (and that is why he does so belong), and who participates in reason so far as to apprehend it but not to possess it. (1254b20)

Yet, immediately after this line of argument, the text moves to acknowledge the justice of those who argue that slavery is not a natural condition. Noting that the bodies of slaves should be markedly different from those of the free, Aristotle observes that they often are not:

> The intention of nature is to make the bodies of freemen and of slaves different – the latter strong for necessary service, the former erect

and unserviceable for such occupations, but serviceable for a life of citizenship ... though as a matter of fact often the very opposite comes about – slaves have the bodies of freemen and freemen the souls only. (1254b30)

Like the Hippolytus of Euripides's tragedy named for him, who wishes he could purchase children with precious metals, their worth determined by their price, so Aristotle wishes that free persons' bodies were as distinguished for their beauty as are the statues of the gods, but resigns himself to the fact that beauty of soul is less apparent to the eye than beauty of the body.

All this leads Aristotle to conclude that those who argue against natural slavery are wrong. He sees the possibility of persons who are enslaved not by nature, barbarians or not, but rather by law, or custom (*nomos*). He admits that some wars may be unjust, and that the captive of such a war might be unjustly enslaved: 'persons reputed of the highest nobility are slaves and the descendants of slaves if they happen to be taken prisoners of war and sold.' (1255a25) But this argument, he says, is used in support of the view that barbarians are natural slaves, Greeks not: 'there exist certain persons who are essentially slaves everywhere and certain others who are so nowhere.' (1255a30) This issue is developed in the later philosophical tradition, which in some schools moves away from the social circumstances of the subject of philosophy, to focus on his inner life. Those who are free in their souls can be tortured without suffering, enslaved without losing their freedom. Cynics, Epicureans and Stoics, the post-Socratic schools who urge a philosophical way of life, reflect on this question and encourage their adherents to develop an indifference to shackles and bondage. The true philosopher is free everywhere.

After this digression, Aristotle returns to another definition of the slave: 'the slave is a part of the master – he is, as it were, a part of the body, alive but yet separated from it.' (1255b10) He goes on to note that there is a science of mastery, and a science, an *episteme*, of slavery: 'the latter being the sort of knowledge that used to be imparted by the professor at Syracuse (for there used to be a man there who for a fee gave lessons to slaves (*paidas*))' [translation modified]. Excited by the possibility of the development of a further branch of knowledge, Aristotle goes on to discuss the branches of such a science, and then moves on the science of acquiring slaves, 'the just acquiring of slaves, being like a sort of warfare or hunting.' (1255b35)

The prestige and status of Aristotle as philosopher and political theorist survived into the Roman period and long after, into the Islamic world and the European middle ages. He set the terms of debates concerning slavery for millennia.[12] As the great classical historian Moses I. Finley wrote concerning the philosophical tradition that followed Aristotle's work on slavery:

> And after Aristotle? The simple answer is that he produced not only the first but also the last formal, systematic analysis of the subject in antiquity, so far as we know. Post–Aristotelian ethical philosophy was marked by a clean break between morality and society, by the location of virtue firmly within the individual soul, and by a consequent insistence on indifference to such externals as social status, including personal freedom in the legal sense.[13]

The Aristotelian legacy on the question of natural slavery endures through the modern age of racialised slavery. As Carl J. Richard observes in his work on the founders of the United States, Thomas Jefferson, involved in the debates concerning the constitution, adapted 'Aristotle's "natural slave" to the American context by making him black.' (97)

As mentioned earlier, some of the Roman Stoics, followers at a great distance of the earlier, more utopian thinkers like the Greek Zeno, considered slavery to be a trivial aspect of the world, unrelated to the true freedom of the soul, which could as easily reside in the body of a slave as in that of an emperor. The Roman Republican orator Cicero, for example, in his work called *Stoic Paradoxes*, presents Stoic ideas in a form useful for everyday life and perhaps even as embellishment for rhetoric. In the fifth of his paradoxes, he considers the Stoic doctrine that 'only the wise man is free, and that every foolish man is a slave.'[14] Following the logic of the

Stoics, he agrees that 'if slavery means, as it does mean, the obedience of a broken and abject spirit that has no volition of its own, who would deny that all light-minded and covetous people and indeed all the vicious are really slaves?' (5.35) A man subject to the command of a woman is likewise a slave, 'a very vile slave,' as is anyone who takes excessive pleasure in works of art. With an indifferent and comic use of the notion of slavery, Cicero condemns the art-lover:

> As in the household those who handle articles of that sort or dust or oil or sweep or sprinkle them do not hold the most honourable rank of slavery, so in the state those who have given themselves up to coveting that sort of thing occupy almost the lowest place in the slave-order itself. (5. 37)

Another is enslaved to money: 'what nod from a rich old man without children does it not attend to?' (39); another to the ambition for state office, military appointments and governerships. Finally, some are enslaved to fear, fearing a guilty conscience, the talk of others who know too much, a judge. The notion of slavery throughout this discourse has become entirely a matter of metaphor; the presence of real slaves, serving, attending, living and dying in bondage to a cruel or a merciful master, barely surfaces in the text.

The Stoic Seneca argued that the soul of a slave could never be subject to a master's violence and coercion, although his body be tortured. For this subject of the Roman emperor, all human beings were to some degree subjugated by their mortal condition, and only the soul could be truly free. In the 'moral essay' called *De Clementia*, 'On Mercy,' addressed to the emperor Nero, Seneca discusses the remission of punishment, the nature of mercy and how the mind can be led to adopt the virtue of mercy, stressing throughout the indispensable importance of mercy for the sovereign. He points to the vastness of Rome, immense in comparison to the tiny compass of the Greek city-state, and to how few persons there achieve moral perfection:

Consider this city, in which the throng that streams ceaselessly through its widest streets is crushed to pieces whenever anything gets in the way to check its course as it streams like a rushing torrent, – this city in which the seating space of three theatres is required at one time, in which is consumed all the produce of the plough from every land; consider how great would be the loneliness and the desolation of it if none should be left but those whom strict judge would acquit. (*On Mercy*, 1. 6.1)[15]

He urges the reader, the emperor, to show mercy in his handling of human beings, even captives and purchased slaves:

Even slaves have the right of refuge at the statue of a god; and although the law allows anything in dealing with a slave, yet in dealing with a human being there is an extreme which the right common to all living creatures refuses to allow. Who did not hate Vedius Pollio even more than his own slaves did, because he would fatten his lampreys on human blood, and order those who had for some reason incurred his displeasure to be thrown into his fish-pond – or why not say his snake-preserve? The monster! He deserved to die a thousand deaths, whether he threw his slaves as food to lampreys he meant to eat, or whether he kept lampreys only to feed them on such food. (*On Mercy*, 1.18.1–2)

The Stoic Seneca is repelled at the cruelty of Vedius Pollio, yet his emphasis falls on the proper behavior of the sovereign rather than urging freedom for slaves, finding fault with those masters who did not practice the simplicity and humility appropriate to a Stoic soul. He did not himself live without slaves, and, of course, this is one consequence of the doctrine that social position in a slave society is a matter of indifference for the philosophically enlightened. There is no need to argue for abolition.

David Brion Davis describes the Roman legacy of the Aristotelian ideas concerning slavery and freedom and the impact of Stoic developments:

According to the jurists Florentinus and Ulpian, slavery was a manifest departure from the *jus naturale*, but was sanctioned by the *jus gentium*. It was the single instance, Ulpian said, of a conflict between the principles of nature and the common law of nations. This sense of tension, inherited from the Stoics, was passed on to the Institutes of Justinian, and thence to the jurisprudence of Western civilization.[16]

And Moses Finley emphasizes the continuity of ordinary Roman thinking on the question of slavery with Aristotle's views, which briefly acknowledged the possibility that slavery was not a natural phenomenon, while treating it as if it were, and that it was the natural condition of the barbarian, that is, the ethnic other: 'That is the implication . . . underlying the commonplace in Roman Republican speeches that Jews, Syrians, Lydians, Medes, indeed all Asiatics, are "born to slavery."'[17] In the paradigm of Greek-Roman vs. barbarian, citizen vs. slave, the racialised others of early modern colonized Africa were easily substituted.

Slavery in the New Testament and in Christianity

The books assembled in the canon of the New Testament were written in the Roman Empire, a polity deeply committed to slave acquisition, sale, trading and employment in domestic, agricultural and other varieties of labour. The Christians, first Jews who were followers of Jesus, usually accept Roman ideas of the natural inevitability of slavery.[18] They also often adopt the attitudes expressed in the Hebrew Bible, especially the notion that the believer is an '*ebed*, a 'slave' of his or her god; in the text of the New Testament '*ebed*, translated into English as both 'slave' and 'servant', becomes *doulos*, unequivocally 'slave,' in Greek.

Slaves surround the characters of New Testament narratives, just as they do in the households of their polytheistic Greek and Roman neighbours, and slaves were among the early converts from Judaism and from polytheism. We hear of the slave of the high priest in Matthew 26. 51. The parable of the talents in Matthew 25 concerns a master who departs on a journey, entrusting money to them; he punishes the slave who makes no profit and says, in words that echo the fate of the poorly dressed wedding guest in 22, 'As for this worthless slave, throw him into the outer darkness, where there will be weeping and gnashing of teeth.' (Matthew 25. 30) The narrative assumes the presence of slaves in the household.

In a parable that underlines the metaphorical slavery of the believer to his god, Jesus tells another story of a wedding guest to illustrate the necessity of readiness for the kingdom of god:

> 'Be dressed for action and have your lamps lit; be like those who are waiting for their master to return from the wedding banquet, so that they may open the door for him as soon as he comes and knocks. Blessed are those slaves whom the master finds alert when he comes. . . .' (Luke 12.35–37)

These references to slavery, although they take for granted the institution of slavery in the culture of Judaea in the first centuries BCE and CE, often allow the listener to identify not only with the master, but also with the slave. Later interpretation, by abolitionists and by pro-slavery writers, emphasizes different aspects of the tradition. In an argument discussed by J. Albert Harrill, in his *Slaves in the New Testament*, Christian abolitionists cited 'the seed growing secretly' approach, that is, 'to find a kernel in the gospel and to make that kernel control biblical interpretation.' (170) Jesus said, 'Do unto others as you would have do unto you,' (Matthew 7:12 and Luke 6:31); although he himself did not condemn slavery, this kernel would develop over time, Jesus expecting it would 'grow in secret throughout church history until its flowering in the present, nineteenth-century abolitionist Christianity':

> Charismatic abolition ministers . . . argued that Jesus planted this kernel of egalitarianism knowing its slow, covert growth would eventually destroy slavery . . . The seed-growing-secretly theory interpreted slavery, like polygamy and divorce, to have been part of the previous

Hebrew 'dispensation' whose divine sanction ended with the advent of Jesus and the Christian 'dispensation.' (170)

Thus both anti-slavery and pro-slavery thinkers found justification for their positions in the Bible, even where there were in fact no abolitionist views expressed.

The letters of the New Testament address more directly than do the gospels the issue of slavery. Famously, the disciple Paul calls himself a *doulos*, a slave, in a formulation that echoes the Hebrew Bible's denomination of the believer as a slave or servant of the god Jahweh-Elohim-Adonai. In the address to the Romans, as a preface to his letter, Paul begins:

Paul, a servant of Jesus Christ, called to be an apostle, set apart for the gospel of God . . . (Romans 1.1)

As in the translation of '*ebed* in the Hebrew text, word choice in English can distort the sense of the original epistle. The word used here, and translated as 'servant,' is *doulos*, 'slave.'[19] The letter to the community in Philippi begins 'Paul and Timothy, *servants* of Christ Jesus' in the translation, *douloi*, 'slaves,' in Greek.

Paul claimed famously that the gospel of Jesus had abolished the opposition between slave and free: 'There is no longer Jew or Greek, there is no longer slave or free, there is no longer male and female; for all of you are one in Christ Jesus.' (Galatians 3.28)[20] Yet many of the letters composed by him, or by others who use his name, seek to regulate the specific conduct appropriate to slaves and masters in the new Christian communities.

Slaves, obey your earthly masters with fear and trembling, in single-ness of heart, as you obey Christ; not only while being watched, and in order to please them, but as slaves of Christ . . . (Ephesians 6.5–6)

These sentiments are echoed in Titus: 'Tell slaves to be submissive to their masters and to give satisfaction in every respect; they are not to talk back, not to pilfer, but to show complete and perfect fidelity (9–10), and in First Peter, in a characteristic list of commands directed to men, husbands, wives and slaves: 'Slaves, accept the authority of your masters with all deference, not only those who are kind and gentle but also those who are harsh.' (2.18)[21]

In perhaps the most-often cited of New Testament passages concerning slaves, Paul writes from prison to Philemon concerning Onesimos, Philemon's fugitive slave. What he asks of Philemon is not entirely clear; the letter was used by pro-slavery and anti-slavery polemicists alike in the modern period, especially with regard to the Fugitive Slave Law of the United States in the antebellum period, a law 'nullified' by a jury in Massachusetts, which refused to obey the law requiring that an escaped slave who had traveled north to slave-free states be returned to the south and to his slavemaster. This letter provides remarkable insight into the everyday life of master and slave in the first century CE. Paul sends the slave back to Philemon, but suggests that he might serve Paul still with his master's consent: 'I wanted to keep him with me, so that he might be of service to me in your place during my imprisonment for the gospel; but I preferred to do nothing without your consent, in order that your good deed might be voluntary and not something forced.' (Philemon 1. 13–14) Is he hinting that the slave could serve him, Paul, as his slave, or that Philemon should free him and let him be Paul's servant? Scholars differ on this point. But the pro-slavery activists of North America fixed on the fact that Paul returned the fugitive slave to his master.

Ante-bellum Arguments for Slavery in North America

Arguments for slavery in the Spanish colonies depended to some degree on Biblical justifications, as did the polemic against such slavery. On the *encomiendas*, the plantations of Latin South America worked first by indigenous peoples, compelled to labour by the 1513 Law of Burgos, which defended the colonizers' practices by citing the precedents of the invasion and conquest of Canaan in the Hebrew Bible, the god of the Bible's annihilation of Sodom, and the New Testament text Matthew 22.1–14, Jesus's account of the wedding feast where the master commands his servant to throw a guest not dressed in a wedding robe 'into the outer darkness . . . For many are called, but few are chosen.' The indigenous people of New Spain were the many, the barbarians, justly conquered by the Spanish invaders. Like the later abolitionists of the northern states of North America, the Dominican friar Bartolome de las Casas, in his *In Defense of the Indians* of 1550, argued rather that the overriding message of Jesus in the New Testament was 'love,' not enslavement.

The slave holders, slave owners, of the southern colonies and the southern states of North America, knew well, and used the ancient ideologies concerning slavery to justify their ownership of the Africans brought to labour on their plantations to replace indentured servants from the old world, or indigenous labourers, from the seventeenth to the nineteenth centuries. They appealed to the antiquity of the practice of slavery, which seemed to naturalize it, make it an inevitable feature of human societies. They saw it as an element of the most noble societies of the past, those of Jerusalem, Athens and Rome, an element that guaranteed the liberty of the free and allowed for the development of the highest degree of civilization. And they saw it as a necessary stage in the evolution of inferior races, or an eternal obligation to the inferiors, to guide them in a life in which their own capacities were inadequate for survival and flourishing. They rarely discussed the economic motives, the profit derived from the exploitation of their slaves, and also failed to recognize that, in fact, their economy may have been permanently damaged by its reliance on the labour-intensive forms of plantation life, which prevented them from ever developing an industrial base like the north's, which allowed the northern states after the civil war to flourish and achieve economic dominance in the post-war years.

The argument that enslavement actually improved the lot of the enslaved, an echo of the Aristotelian view, was one often resorted to in debates, especially as the abolitionist movement in the north gathered strength. John

C. Calhoun, for example, offered these words as 'facts' in a speech given in the US Senate on February 6, 1837:

> Never before has the black race of Central Africa, from the dawn of history to the present day, attained a condition so civilized and so improved, not only physically, but morally and intellectually. It came among us in a low, degraded and savage condition, and in the course of a few generations it has grown up under the fostering care of our institutions, reviled as they have been, to its present comparatively civilized condition. This, with the rapid increase of numbers, is conclusive proof of the general happiness of the race, in spite of all the exaggerated tales to the contrary.[22]

Such 'facts' were in Calhoun's speech coupled with a denunciation of the capitalist north, site of 'a conflict between labour and capital', 'the eager pursuit of gain which overspreads the land, and which absorbs every faculty of the mind and every feeling of the heart.' (13–14) He sees the passion of avarice around him, and sets against it the noble impulses of his own kind, who seek only to improve the lot of the blacks and have quiet and stability instead of conflict.

The Americans relied on the Bible, Old Testament and New, to provide a rationale for the inevitability of slavery in civilized life. In The *Bible Argument: Or, Slavery in the Light of Divine Revelation*, published in Richmond, Virginia, in 1856 and again in Atlanta, Georgia in 1860, Thornton Stringfellow wrote a careful gloss on the Biblical justifications for slavery. He goes back to Noah, in Genesis 9. 25–27, who curses Canaan, and gives mastery of the children of Ham to Shem and Japheth. In Stringfellow's reading of the Bible, the Hebrew god connected the very existence of slavery 'with prophetic tokens of special favour, to those who should be slave owners or masters.' (McKitrick, 87) Abraham held slaves, bought in Haran. Hagar the Egyptian slave, mother of Ishmael, is urged to return to her mistress by an angel. Slaves are 'inventoried as property which *God had given to Abraham.*' (89) Against the abolitionists the author cites numerous passages in which servants are property, and he goes on to list other slave owners, holding 'servants' as property: Moses and Job. Joseph is 'a friend to absolute slavery.' And throughout the Hebrew Bible's account of the patriarchal age, under the Mosaic law, 'there is not a reproof uttered against the institution of *involuntary slavery*.' He accuses the abolitionists of misreading the Bible when they argue against slavery, and he points out that, although making hereditary slaves of the Hebrews themselves was forbidden, enslaving people of another nation was never prohibited, and had been, as noted earlier in this chapter, urged on the earliest patriarch by the god himself. And he goes on to show that 'Jesus Christ recognized this institution as one that was lawful among men, and regulated its relative duties.' (94) Here he cites the letters to the Ephesians, Colossians and Corinthians, as well as Peter, and he finds evidence, again against the abolitionist view, that Jesus himself, according to the testimony of Paul, said that a slave should serve even an unbelieving master. William Ruffin, in *The Political Economy of Slavery*, published in Washington in 1853, also cites the wonders of the past, going back to the Hebrew Bible to find his examples: 'it was on this institution of domestic slavery that was erected the admirable and beneficent (sic) mastership and government of the patriarch Abraham.' (McKitrick, 76)

And the pro-slavery polemicists referred often to pagan antiquity and its practices of slaveholding, to demonstrate the superiority of slave-owning societies of the past. James Henry Hammond, in his speech on the admission of Kansas to the Union, in the US Senate in 1858, pointing out the great wealth derived from the cultivation of cotton, saying 'cotton is king,' uses Cicero to argue for the inevitability of slavery:

> In all social systems there must be a class to do the menial duties, to perform the drudgery of life . . . It constitutes the very mud-sill of society . . . Fortunately for the South, she found a race adapted to that purpose to her hand. A race inferior to her own . . . we use them for our purpose, and call them slaves. We found them slaves by the common 'consent of mankind,' which, according to Cicero, '*lex naturae est*.'[23]

Thomas Dew, at William and Mary College, who published a review of the debate in the Virginia Legislature of 1831 and 1832, summed up the rationale derived from ancient examples:

> We must recollect that the *laws* of Lycurgus were promulgated, the sublime eloquence of Demosthenes and Cicero was heard, and the glorious achievements of Epaminondas and Scipio were witnessed, in countries where slavery existed— . . . .[24]

He believes that slavery is of the *order of nature* (33), and therefore cannot be legislated away. The 'sociologist for the South' George Fitzhugh argued that 'to [slavery] Greece and Rome, Egypt and Judea and all the other distinguished States of antiquity, were indebted for their great prosperity and high civilization . . .'

> But this high civilization and domestic slavery did not merely co-exist, they were cause and effect. Every scholar whose mind is at all imbued with ancient history and literature, sees that Greece and Rome were indebted to this institution alone for the taste, the leisure and the means to cultivate their heads and their hearts . . . .[25]

Fitzhugh, like Dew, condemns the north as a site of free labour and capitalism, thrifty and utilitarian, producing men like Ben Franklin with his 'penny saved is a penny earned,' but not poets, orators, sculptors and artists. In contrast, 'domestic slavery in the Southern States has produced the same results in elevating the character of the master that it did in Greece and Rome.'

The analogies made between the different regions of the United States and the different states of classical antiquity, Athens, Sparta and Rome, differed from north to south. Carl J. Richard notes that 'Antebellum southerners seized upon Athens, now rehabilitated by pro-democratic historians, as a model society. Southern social critics attributed the greatness of the polis to slavery.' (241) Slavery revealed the necessity of freedom to citizens, and gave them leisure for cultural development. The Southern states founded cities like Athens, Georgia, site of the University of Georgia, to emphasize the kinship between themselves and these ancient models.

In her book *The Culture of Classicism: Ancient Greece and Rome in American Intellectual Life 1780–1910*, Caroline Winterer discusses the early admiration for the states of Greek and Roman antiquity, which diverged when tensions began to rise over the question of slavery, especially after Nat Turner's rebellion of 1831.[26] The southerners began to invoke ancient Greece, 'and especially ancient Athens, to justify the nobility of a slave society.' (74) They saw parallels between the Greek climate, and its city-states, with the South. Intellectuals in the south cited Aristotle and Herodotus to show that slavery was beneficial for both slave owner and slave. A shift from the focus on Rome to Greece, characteristic in the ante-bellum period, took particular shape in the south around the issue of Athenian slavery and Athens' philosophers and historians. Analogies were made casting 'the North as an overweening Sparta to the South's more democratic Athens, or a licentious Athens to the South's more socially conservative Sparta, or to a modern-day Macedonia threatening Athenian liberties.' (75) In any case, the issue of slavery in Greek and Roman antiquity made these a convenient model for the South's self-fashioning in relation to the northern states, as the war approached.

Ancient ideologies, from both the Hebraic and the Hellenic traditions, helped the pro-slavery thinkers of the antebellum period in the United States formulate their arguments justifying the continuation of slavery in the south, and its extension to the new states that were on the verge of being admitted to the union. In the form of scripture, both the old testament and the new, Southern writers cited evidence of the divine approval of slavery. In addition to support from the new sciences of scientific history and a proto-anthropology, and in direct contradiction to the abolitionists' claims concerning the immorality and uncharitable nature of slave-holding, based often on Christian morality, they discovered support from the practices of the divinity himself in Genesis and Exodus. And in the New

Testament, in the words of Paul himself, they accumulated further justification for the peculiar institution that was chattel, plantation slavery in the south. Beyond these religious justifications, sanctified by their origins in the sacred books of Christianity, and therefore more precious than any new science or even an enlightenment view of sympathy or universal humanism, they found support in the texts of ancient Greece and Rome. Aristotle's view that slavery for some was natural, and indeed an improvement on life without a master, sustained in Roman practices and in Roman law, found eager readers in the American south. Not only was the greatest philosopher of antiquity a slave owner himself, who made slavery an integral element in his theorization of politics, but he also provided a rationale flexible enough to be adapted easily to the racialised slavery of the Americas. If 'barbarians' were natural slaves and benefited from the mastery of the Greeks, then this natural hierarchy of master and slave conformed beautifully to the difference between white and black, American and African, in the new circumstances of modern slavery.

CHAPTER IV

ANCIENT SLAVERY

'What if some god were to lift one of these men, his fifty or more slaves, and his wife and children out of the city and deposit him with his slaves and other property in a deserted place, where no free person could come to his assistance? How frightened would he be that himself and his wife and children would be killed by the slaves?'

'Very frightened indeed.'

'And wouldn't he be compelled to fawn on some of his own slaves, promise them lots of things, and free them, even though he didn't want to? And wouldn't he himself have become a panderer to slaves?'

'He'd have to or else be killed.'

Plato, *Republic* 578e-579a

As the great ancient historian Moses Finley wrote: 'I should say that there was no action or belief or institution in Graeco-Roman antiquity that was not one way or other affected by the possibility that someone involved *might be* a slave.' In this chapter, after beginning with a brief look at slavery in ancient Israel, I will focus on the history of slavery in ancient Greece and Rome, on the everyday life and interactions of slaves and free persons in these societies, and on some literary texts that offer glimpses of how the free viewed slaves in the world of so-called 'pagan' antiquity.

Slavery in Israel

The evidence of the everyday existence of slaves in early Israel is scanty and must rely for the most part on the textual evidence in the books of the Hebrew Bible. One episode that involves a slave is that mentioned earlier, concerning an Egyptian slave of Abraham, Hagar. Sarai orders Abraham to 'go in' to her slave-girl, so that she Sarai can have children through Hagar. Hagar had a child, but then looked with contempt on her mistress, and Sarai, with Abram's permission, 'dealt harshly with her, and she ran away from her.' (Genesis 16.6) But an angel comes to Hagar and tells her to submit to Sarai, and promises to 'multiply [her] offspring that they cannot be counted for multitude.' (16.10) This son, though, will be 'a wild ass of a man, with his hand against everyone, and everyone's hand against him; and he shall live at odds with all his kin.' (16.12) Then the god makes his covenant with Abram, who becomes Abraham, and his wife, who becomes Sarah, and he and Ishmael and 'all the slaves born in his house or bought with his money' (17.23) are circumcised. And Sarah conceives her own son, the free-born Isaac, and turns against the slave-born Ishmael: 'Sarah saw the son of Hagar the Egyptian, whom she had borne to Abraham, playing with her son Isaac. So she said to Abraham, "Cast out this slave woman with her son; for the son of this slave woman shall not inherit along with my son Isaac."' (Genesis 21.9) Hagar is cast out, wanders in the wilderness, is dying of thirst and leaves her child so she will not have to watch him die. But an angel of the god calls to her from heaven, and she finds water, after a promise that the boy will make a great nation. (21.14–19) He grows up in the wilderness, and marries an Egyptian. And he enters the Quran.

The story of the slave Hagar points to the presence of foreign, non-Israelite slaves among the community of those who eventually, at least mythically, survive enslavement themselves to the Egyptians and go on to found their own nation in the land of the Canaanites. And to possess slaves, both Israelite and not, in their new land. This particular narrative, as mentioned earlier, has later consequences in the struggles between modern-day Jewish Israelis and Muslim Palestinians, who trace their 'racial' or tribal differences back to this moment, although according to Islamic tradition the aborted sacrifice according was of Abraham's son Ishmael, rather than of Isaac.

Slavery in Greece[1]

The Mycenaeans, Indo-European predecessors to archaic and classical Greek society, held slaves, the word for slave, *doeri*, like later *douloi*, found in their records in the script called Linear B. There were slaves in the long period of time during which the Homeric poems the *Iliad* and the *Odyssey* were composed; scholars assume that some of the information contained in them goes back to the twelfth century BCE and even earlier, while they may have been assembled in a form more like that we have now in the eighth century BCE, when literacy was being restored or revived in the Greek world. The women of Troy, in the *Iliad*, fear enslavement, even the queen of Priam, Hecuba, and her daughter-in-law Andromache, wife of the great Trojan hero Hektor. In the *Odyssey*, the household of Odysseus, which awaits his return from the victory at Troy, contains many slaves, including the noble swineherd Eumaios, who himself owned a slave. Eumaios, born the son of a king, recounts his story to the disguised Odysseus: His nurse was promised a return to her Phoenician home by Phoenician traders who visited Eumaios's island. She stole him from his father's house and took him to the Phoenicians' ship. The woman dies as they sail from Syria, and the traders sell him to Laertes, father of Odysseus. Eumaios is loyal to the memory of Odysseus, who he fears has perished in so many years away from home. He is a faithful retainer, longing for the return of his master, and when Odysseus reveals himself, he aids him in recovering his property and family from the predatory suitors who surround Penelope.

Another vividly portrayed slave character is Eurykleia, once nurse herself to Odysseus.

She was the daughter of Ops the son of Peisenor, and Laertes had bought her long ago with his own possessions when she was still in her first youth, and gave twenty oxen for her, and he favoured her in his own house as much as his own devoted wife, but never slept with her, for fear of his wife's anger. (*Odyssey* 1.429–33)[2]

As is usual in aristocratic texts, these named slaves are faithful, noble and devoted to their masters, perhaps because they had once been free and aristocrats themselves. Twelve of the fifty women slaves of the house, who had been taught by Eurykleia 'how to endure their own slavery' (22.423), had taken to immorality with the suitors of Odysseus's wife, Penelope, and were punished after they had cleaned up the mess from Odysseus's slaughter of the suitors. Telemachos, Odysseus's son, gives them a mass hanging:

> . . . like thrushes, who spread their wings, or pigeons, who have flown
> into a snare set up for them in a thicket, trying to find a resting place,
> but the sleep given them was hateful, so their heads were all in a line,
> and each had her neck caught fast in a noose, so that their death
> would be most pitiful. They struggled with their feet for a little, not
> for very long. (22.467–472)

The house of Odysseus is now cleansed of dishonour and infidelity and ready for him to reveal himself to the wife who has waited twenty years for his return.

In Athens, the city concerning which we have most evidence in the classical period, a great increase in the owning of slaves occurred in the sixth century BCE. The politician Solon apparently responded to class conflict in the city, where all citizens had some right to equality with all others, given the myth of autochthony that posited a common birth from the earth itself for the Athenians, descended from a failed rape of Athena by Hephaistos. His seed was brushed from Athena's garment to the earth, and the ancestor of the Athenians was born from this triple union. The citizens of the city, at the beginning of the sixth century, seem to have been agitating against an increase in aristocratic power and wealth. Poorer citizens were mortgaging their land to the rich, losing control of it, and being forced to sell themselves into slavery, even to other cities in Greece and perhaps beyond. The text called *The Athenian Constitution*, attributed to Aristotle but probably by a student of his, lays out the story of this early phase of Athenian history:

> ... there was strife for a long time between the notables and the masses. For the Athenians' constitution was oligarchic in all other respects, and in particular the poor were enslaved to the rich – themselves and their children and their wives. The poor were called dependants and sixth-parters, since it was for the rent of a sixth that they worked the fields of the rich. All the land was in the hands of a few, and if the poor failed to pay their rents both they and their children were liable to seizure. All loans were made on the security of the person until the time of Solon; he was the first champion of the people. The harshest and bitterest aspect of the constitution for the masses was the fact of their enslavement, though they were discontented on other grounds too; it could be said that there was nothing in which they had a share.[3] (*Ath. Pol.* 2)

Solon, chosen as 'lawgiver,' put a stop to the mortgaging of their lands, and a form of share-cropping, the sixth-parting, that impoverished them, forbade the enslavement of Athenian citizens, and even reclaimed those who had been sold abroad and had forgotten their own dialect. And he boasts of these accomplishments in his poetry:

> My purpose was to bring my scattered people back
> together. Where did I fall short of my design?
> I call to witness at the judgment seat of time
> one who is noblest, mother of Olympian
> divinities, and greatest of them all, Black Earth.
> I took away the mortgage stones stuck in her breast,

and she, who went a slave before, is now set free.
Into this sacred land, our Athens, I brought back
a throng of those who had been sold, some by due law,
though others wrongly; some by hardship pressed to escape
the debts they owed; and some of these no longer spoke
Attic, since they had drifted wide around the world,
while those in the country had the shame of slavery
upon them, and they served their masters' moods in fear.
These I set free; and I did this by strength of hand,
welding right law with violence to a single whole.[4]

Earth herself, the goddess and the sacred land of Attica, had been gouged, fettered and marked by the signs of slavery, now eradicated through Solon's violence, or threats of violence.

After the reforms of Solon, Athenian citizens never again suffered the social death and dishonour of enslavement by their fellow-citizens, and they reminded one another of this special status frequently. Slavery became a constant theme of literal and metaphorical political discourse. And the Athenians then began to rely more heavily on slaves from elsewhere, from other Greek cities and from 'barbarian' sources, people kidnapped like Eumaios, captured in war or by pirates, sold by slave merchants, exposed in a form of attempted infanticide and reclaimed by slavers or born and raised as slave children in their own households, sometimes fathered by the master of the house.

The numbers of such slaves, and their relative numbers vis-à-vis the citizens and other free persons, such as metics, free people but non-Athenians, is difficult to gauge. Most scholars estimate that the number of slaves was about a quarter of the population, although there were circumstances where whole regions were enslaved, as communities. Households included domestic slaves, slaves worked in manufacturing, making pottery and weapons, and in the fields. The city of Athens itself owned Scythian slaves, archers who served as its police force and who supervised the assembly of the citizens in their democratic meetings. In the silver mines of Laurion, in Attica, the city-state of Athens, there may have been up to 30,000 slaves in the fourth century BCE. But there were no immense plantations worked by slaves, as there were later in Rome and in the modern Americas.

Sparta and a few other city-states had, as mentioned above, entire populations of their neighbours in forms of bondage, called in the case of Sparta 'helotry.'[5] Paul Cartledge sums up the importance of the enslaved surrounding communities in the classical period:

> These Helots are the single most important human fact about ancient Sparta. Divided into two main groups, the Messenians to the west of Mt Taygetus and the Laconians to its East, the Helots provided the Spartans with the economic basis of their unique lifestyle. They vastly outnumbered the full Spartan citizens, who in self-defence called themselves Hoimoioi or 'Similars' . . . The Spartans were exceptionally successful masters, keeping the Helots in subjection for more than three centuries. But they did so at considerable cost.[6]

The Spartans lived in fear of slave revolts, and devoted themselves to the task of mastering the helots, making their society a military camp in which all male citizens served only as soldiers. There were other such communities, dominated and subjugated by their neighbours, in Thessaly, Heraclea on the Black Sea, Crete and in the Sicilian city of Syracuse, where indigenous people called *killyrioi* worked the land of the wealthy before they were overpowered in a democratic revolution. The slaves of the Athenians were scattered, never concentrated in large numbers on plantations, or in such communities as the helots' where family could to some degree be sustained, although the Spartan *homoioi* could kill any helot without legal consequences.

Herodotus describes the vulnerability of those captured and enslaved by slave merchants, and cites the case of one Hermotimos, who was a trusted slave of Xerxes, emperor of the Persians.

He was taken prisoner in a war, put up for sale, and bought by a man from Chios called Panionius. Now, Panionius made a living in the most atrocious way imaginable. What he used to do was acquire good-looking boys, castrate them, and take them to Sardis and Ephesus, where he would offer them for sale at very high prices; in foreign countries eunuchs command higher prices than whole men on account of their complete reliability. (8.105)

Hermotimos becomes the emperor's most trusted eunuch, lures Panionius to Atarneus and takes his revenge. He has Panionius's four sons brought into the room where they are waiting, makes the father castrate his sons, and then forces them to castrate their father. Chios was long associated with slavery; Athenaeus, a compiler of the third century CE, claims, based on earlier historians' work, that chattel slavery was invented on the island.

Slave dress differed from that of the free. Slaves had cruder, rougher hair-cuts, sometimes wore garments made of roughly sewn animal skins, and were often different in skin and hair colour from the Greeks themselves. Barbarian slaves seem, for example, often to have had reddish or blonde hair, in contrast with the free citizens, and bore such names as Xanthias, 'tawny,' in reference to a lighter colouring than the Greeks'. Slave prostitutes seem to have worn snoods on their hair that mark them as slaves in vase paintings. Others had names referring to their place of origin, such as Thratta, 'female Thracian.' These features of slave life, along with sexual vulnerability, the threat of castration, for example, or rape or use by the master, correspond to the markers of slavery adduced by Orlando Patterson, in that they are signs of social death, and dishonour. An American slave owner, Henry Laurens, called his slaves 'Tully,' for Cicero, 'Valerius,' and 'Claudius'; these slaves bear names signifying a loss of their former identity, and perhaps a parodic grandiosity, or an inflating of their masters' status.[7] In the Greek case, their names describe them as objects, defined by colouring or place of origin. On works of art, in aristocratic periods the slaves presented with their masters are often shown as beautiful, serene and dignified. In later more democratic moments and in the monarchic Hellenistic period, slaves no longer shared the elegance of their masters, and are more often shown as smaller than their masters, squatting close to the ground, bearing grotesque features that excite either contempt or pathos in the viewer.[8]

Slaves had some protections afforded by religious sites; they could take sanctuary in temples. After the new year festival of Hekatombaia, where one hundred animals may have been sacrificed to Apollo, the Athenians celebrated the festival of Kronia. Slaves were liberated for the day and feasted with their masters, recalling the age of Kronos, the deposed father of Zeus, the Greeks' sovereign god. The time of Kronos' rule was remembered as a golden age, before labour and pain entered human existence, and some Athenian comedies seem to have alluded to this time when slaves – there were always slaves – dined on bacon and had a less miserable fate.

As an illustration of Moses Finley's remark, that 'there was no action or belief or institution in Graeco-Roman antiquity that was not one way or other affected by the possibility that someone involved *might be* a slave,' I will look at just one legal oration, a speech given in an Athenian lawcourt in the late fifth or early fourth century BCE, to demonstrate the inevitable presence of slaves in every situation in ancient Greece. This is the speech delivered by the Athenian orator Andokides called 'On the Mysteries,' probably from 400 BCE, possibly from 399 BCE. In this speech, delivered to a group of Athenian citizens chosen by lot, as all juries were, he defended himself against a charge of impiety. He had, years before, been accused of religious crimes, of mutilating the Herms and of profaning the Eleusinian Mysteries. Herms were pillars set as markers in the streets of Athens; each had a bearded head at its top and a phallus protruding from its front. Before the departure of an Athenian expedition to the island of Sicily in 415, an adventure of conquest, persons unknown had gone through the city and broken the herms; this was considered a grave sacrilege, offending the god Hermes, who watched over travellers, an offense that could jeopardize the fleet on its expedition to Sicily. As events unfolded, it was learned also that there had been sacrilegious performances of the mysteries of the Attic city of Eleusis, secret mysteries sacred to the goddess Demeter and her daughter

Persephone, or Kore. The parodic performances of the mysteries, which were never to be revealed to the uninitiated, had taken place in Athens itself, and the commander of the fleet sailing to Sicily, the aristocratic Alcibiades, was implicated by witnesses. Andokides recalls these events of years past to clear his name of having informed on fellow-conspirators, and even on his own father. And he cites not only his own innocence, but also laws and decrees passed in the interim that declared an amnesty for past crimes. He defends himself of the earlier accusations, and of later impieties, and also accuses his accusers of self-interest, cowardice and distortion of the facts. Slaves enter into this case at several moments, in ways that illustrate their omnipresence in the circumstances of everyday life in the city of Athens, and also the ways in which they were vulnerable to laws that protected the free but left them defenseless.

Andokides begins his narrative by recalling the initial discovery of the crimes, when someone at the Assembly of the citizens names one of the commanders of the fleet, as having profaned the mysteries:

Alcibiades the general, as I shall prove to you, has been performing the Mysteries with others at a private house; and if you vote to give immunity to the person to whom I tell you to, a servant of one of the men present here, though he is uninitiated, will tell you the Mysteries.[9] (11)

Alcibiades denied the charges, and the presidents of the Assembly go themselves and bring back the witness, a servant of Alcibiades named Andromachus, who confirms the story, adding that Alcibiades himself was one of the actual performers. '. . . but others were also present and saw what was done, including some slaves – himself, his brother, Hicesius the piper and Meletus's slave.' (12)

This testimony damns Alcibiades, but it also, incidentally, makes clear the dangers of slave presence in the households of the free. Slaves attended the symposia, waited on the symposiasts, poured their wine, were available sexually, for example, but they also saw and listened to everything that occurred in the households. To use James Scott's terms, deference and obedience characterize the public transcript, shadowed by a 'hidden transcript,' one exchanged among people of dependent status often concealing rage and a thirst for vengeance. For Alcibiades's slave to betray him to the Assembly is for him to act publicly, overcoming the inhibitions to keep the transcript hidden.[10]

Aristophanes, the Athenian writer of comic drama, alludes to these matters in scenes he stages in which slaves, played by actors, speak to one another out of the presence of their masters. In the *Frogs*, for example, Xanthias, slave of the god Dionysos who had been pretending to be Dionysos disguised in turn as Herakles, exchanges confidences with the slave of the underworld judge Aiakos:

SLAVE: I swear by Zeus the Savior, that master of yours is a gentleman.

XANTHIAS: Of course he's a gentleman: a guy who only knows about boozing and balling.

SLAVE: But not to have beaten you as soon as you, the slave, were caught pretending to be the master!

XANTHIAS : Then he'd have regretted it!

SLAVE: Well, you certainly talk like a true slave! I like talking that way myself. . . . it's like nirvana whenever I curse my master behind his back!

XANTHIAS : And what about muttering when you leave the house after getting a heavy beating?

SLAVE: I love that too.

XANTHIAS : And what about meddling?

SLAVE: Positively nonpareil!

XANTHIAS : Ah Zeus of True Kin! And eavesdropping on masters when they're gossiping?

SLAVE: I'm simply mad about it!

XANTHIAS : And what about blabbing it to outsiders?

SLAVE: Who, me?

Why doing that gives me an actual orgasm.[11] (738–53)

The slave of Alcibiades is blabbing about things done in his master's house to outsiders, and the consequences are extremely serious. Alcibiades was stripped of his command, and ordered to stand trial, at risk of death for his impiety. He escaped to the enemy, for a time.

Another slave informant figures in this case. 'Lydus, belonging to Pherecles of Themacus, gave information that Mysteries were performed in the house of his master Pherecles at Themacus.' (17) The father of the speaker is then implicated in the charges, and himself indicts his accuser. And here the issue of the testimony of slaves comes to the fore. It is unclear how the question of torture of slaves was handled in the case of Andromachus, Alcibiades's slave, who eventually received a substantial reward for informing on his master. (27) But Andokides's father urges slave torture, as was customary in the Athenian legal system; testimony from slaves, in almost all cases, was not admissible unless obtained by torture.[12] Andokides's father:

> actually said he never went to Themacus, to see Pherecles, and he urged him to put his slaves to the torture to prove it, and not to refuse to examine people who offered their slaves for torture while compelling people who refused. (22)

The forensic assumption was that slave testimony was true when arrived at through torture and otherwise not. Later in his speech, Andokides himself reminds his audience, the jury, that he proved he could not have been involved in the mutilation of the herms because he had been injured in a horse-riding accident and, although he had agreed to participate, did not. 'To show that this was true, I handed over my slave for torture to prove that I'd been ill and hadn't even been getting up from my bed.' (64) Providing one's slave for torture was a routine procedure, and Aristotle, in his *Rhetoric*, lists torture as one of the methods of proof to be used in legal oratory, although some scholars argue that torture was not routinely practiced but the opportunity merely offered as a proof.

The issue of the torturing of slaves surfaces elsewhere in this fascinating legal document, where it is made clear that the prohibition on torturing citizens is one of those practices serving constantly to distinguish between slave and free. In the hysteria surrounding perceived threats to the state, in the incident of the mutilation of the herms, one participant in a meeting of the democracy, Peisander, says that 'the decree of the year of Scamandrius should be repealed, and those listed should be put on to the wheel, to make sure that all the men were discovered before nightfall. When Mantitheus and Apsephion heard this they went to sit at the altar, begging not to be tortured . . .' (43) The decree in question, of unknown date, but possibly from the sixth century BCE, forbade the torture of Athenian citizens. This protection continually produced the differentiation between slave and free, between those vulnerable to torture if involved even peripherally, accidentally, in a legal matter and those whose bodies were inviolate.

In another passage in which the everyday attitude toward slavery is revealed, an informant clarifies the circumstances in which he happened to see the gathering of a group of conspirators in the herms mutilation episode. Diocleides accuses three hundred citizens of participation in the sacrilege. And he tells the story: 'He had a slave at Laurium, and had to collect a payment. He got up early, mistaking the time, and started walking; there was a full moon.' (38) He spots the mutilators at the theatre of Dionysos and recognizes faces in the moonlight. It turns out, according to Plutarch, that he is a liar, because there was no moon on the night the herms were mutilated. But his excuse about being out very early in the morning reveals another aspect of the everyday practices of slave owners in Athens. His slave had been hired out to work as a miner in Laurion, in the silver mines so profitable to the city, which provided the silver for their coins used all over the Aegean. The fate of the slave-miners was a particularly miserable one; the workers in the mines had notoriously short lives. But their owners received payment for their labours, and so they leased out their slaves for these services.

The last moment in this forensic oration that touches on the question of slavery involves the vulnerability of all free persons to enslavement. In war, and during travel, the free could be taken captive and made slaves; Eumaios provides an early example of kidnapping for slavery, and it was said that Plato himself was captured, held for ransom, and sold as a slave during a voyage to Sicily. In this case, the speaker reminds his audience of jurors that if, as his accusers insist, the gods intended to punish him, they could easily have done so as he travelled by ship.

> 'If they [the gods] thought I'd done them wrong, they wouldn't have let me go unpunished when they had me in the greatest danger. When are people in greater danger than crossing the sea in winter-time? . . . there was a war on. There were always triremes at sea, and pirates too; many people were taken prisoner, lost their possessions, and spent the rest of their lives as slaves.' (137)

Slave-traders and pirates had no qualms about seizing free persons, demanding ransom for them, or enslaving and selling them in such slave depots as the island of Delos. Exposure to such practices was a constant feature of life in Greek antiquity.

In Greek tragedy, characters allude to the possibilities of such a disaster. Especially in those dramas set in and around the city of Troy, besieged, falling and fallen, as it is defeated by the Greeks, the women bemoan their potential destiny as slaves. Although these are ancient narratives, far distant in time from the audience that sits in the theatre of Dionysos in the fifth century BCE, the possibility of enslavement after the defeat of one's city must have haunted them and can recall for a later audience the story of Olaudah Equiano, for one. The Athenians forbade the representation in tragedy of episodes from the recent past and fined Phrynichus, an early tragedian, who had put on stage, probably in 492 BCE, the sufferings of the citizens of Miletus, a sister city of Athens, who had been conquered, the men of the city killed, the women enslaved. Herodotus tells the story of the Persian victory, which had been prophesied by the god Apollo:

> The Persians blockaded Miletus . . . and they reduced the city to slavery, and so events confirmed a prediction the oracle had made about Miletus. . . .

And listen, Miletus, perpetrator of evil deeds: that is when
Many will feed off you and take you as their gleaming prize.
Your wives will wash the feet of a host of long-haired men,
And others will have charge of my temple at Didyma.

This is the fate that overtook Miletus . . . Most of the male population was killed by the Persians (who did have long hair), their women
and children were reduced to slavery, and the shrine at Didyma –
both the temple and the oracle – was plundered and burnt. (*Histories*,
6.18–19)

The metaphor of enslavement is constantly invoked by Greek authors in
discussions of political conflict, within the city, between the city-states and
in relation to the Persians, but the literal fact of enslavement was always
also a possibility.

The mention of such current events as the sack of Miletus was avoided
in fifth century tragedy after Phrynichus's fine, but the issue of enslavement,
represented allegorically in the form of the Trojans especially, recurs
throughout classical drama. Andromache, once wife of Hektor, the greatest
warrior of the Trojans, finds herself, in Euripides's play named for her, a
slave in the possession of Achilles's son, the Greek Neoptolemos.
Andromache has become the slave of her master's new wife, Hermione.
She recalls her 'day of slavery,' the day Troy fell, when her infant son was
thrown alive from the ramparts of the city to his death:

'What a torrent of tears on my cheek the day that I left forever City
and roofs I knew, husband dead in the dust.
Doomed Andromache now! why longer look upon heaven? – Only
a slave, *her* slave – one who oppresses me so
That here to the goddess's shrine I come, a suppliant clutching, Melting
away, all tears, like water welling on rock.'[13] (111–16)

Tragedy abounds in such laments, sung by archaic princesses, by anonymous choruses, by mothers such as Hecuba, who cries, 'I have seen my children die,/ and bound to shame I walk this homeless earth,/ a slave, and see the smoke that leaps up/over Troy.' (*Hecuba*, 822–25) Hecuba takes a violent revenge on her new master, butchering his sons and blinding him.

The brutality and violence of these dramas, which recall events not only of the legendary past, but of the audience's present day, bring home to them the realities of slavery even as they live surrounded by slaves, victims of birth into enslavement, captives of war, persons sold into slavery or captured and kidnapped. The comedies of Aristophanes may speak to the masters' imagination of their slaves' deliberate lethargy, counter-conduct and hidden agendas of resentment and vengeance, but only rarely did Greek slaves join together to threaten en masse the culture of the masters.

There were everyday forms of resistance, of the sort delineated by James Scott. There were denunciations, like that of Alcibiades's slave who accused him of parodying the Eleusinian Mysteries. Slaves from Athens fled in great numbers, according to Thucydides, during the Peloponnesian War, when the Spartans received them in the Attic garrison of Deceleia, occupied by the enemy from 413 to 404 BCE (Thucydides 7. 10, 27–8). But there were no revolts by the chattel slaves of Athens.

Rebellion did occur among the helot communities of the Spartans in the classical period. The Messenians, who had been subjugated by the Spartans in the eighth and seventh centuries BCE, in two wars, never fully accepted Spartan domination, and in 464 BCE, after a huge earthquake, they rebelled and only surrendered after a long siege. The Athenians, who occupied a garrison at Pylos in the Peloponnesus during the Peloponnesian War, encouraged intermittent revolts. And, finally, the Theban general Epaminondas, in the fourth century BCE, helped the Messenians achieve independence from Spartan control; they established a new capital, Messene, and maintained its freedom thereafter. There was also a slave revolt in the mines of Laurion in 103 BCE and at about the same time in Delos, site of the great slave market of the eastern Aegean Sea. Joseph Vogt, author of *Ancient Slavery and the Ideal of Man*, notes that 'The slaves who worked in the mines at

Laureum were able to occupy the fortress of Sunium in the course of their second rebellion, and this gave them a base for their pillaging expeditions through Attica.'[14] These revolts at the silver mines of Attica were part of a wave of slave rebellions of the period, of which more will be said in the following section on Roman slavery, since these revolts occurred in the centuries of transition between Hellenistic, Greek, control of these regions, and the transfer of power into Roman hands.

After the conquest of Greece by Philip II of Macedonia, and the further conquests eastward in Persia, south into Africa, and further east as far as the Indus River and beyond by his heir Alexander, the empire built by the Macedonians disintegrated after Alexander's death. But the great city of Alexandria, in Egypt, founded by Alexander, flourished under the Macedonian Ptolemies, who invented a style of sovereignty fusing their traditions with those of the Pharaohs whom they replaced. And, in the vibrant metropolis that was their capital, a heterogenous population grew up, composed of immigrant Macedonians, Greeks from the islands and the mainland, from Sicily and Magna Graecia, the colonies of the Greek cities in Italy, Nubians from further south in Africa, Judaeans from Southwest Asia, other immigrants from Asia Minor and of course, the Egyptians themselves. The result was a heady mixture of traditions of economic, social, political and literary relationships. The first Greek novels, of this time and later, involve complicated plots implicating romances, travel and slaves, and point to the heterogeneity of the post-Alexander period. The free persons of Alexandria owned many slaves. Although this notice concerning runaway slaves comes from a later period, during the time when Egypt became part of the Roman empire, it suggests the complexity of relationships among kinds of persons from different ethnic communities and between them and their slaves. This is a papyrus, preserved in the sands of Egypt, a declaration made in a census dating from 189 CE:

> Which (property) I am registering in the house-by-house census of the aforementioned village for the 28th year, just completed, of Our Lord Emperor Aurelius Commodus Antoninus Caesar. I (the

declarant) named Isidora, 60(+) years of age, and my slaves [literally 'slave bodies']: Philoumene, 45 years old, and her offspring Dioskouros, 8 years old, and Athenarios, 4 years old; and another slave, Elephantine, offspring of Demetria, 20 years old, and her offspring Eudaimonis, 5 years old, and Isaurous, 1 year old; and another female slave, Helen, who has run away, 68 years old; and Ammonarion, 42 years old, and Herakleia, 38 years old, who have also run away.[15]

This extended household, with its absent fugitive slaves, contained up to ten slaves, most with Greek names like that of their mistress but one, Ammonarion, has a Hellenized Egyptian name. Another runaway slave mentioned in a legal notice is named Sarapion, after the god Sarapis, a synthetic deity concocted by one of the Ptolemies, combining features of Greek with Egyptian gods. (Shaw, 59) Slaves with Greek names may not be in fact of Greek origin, but rather given Greek names by their owners, just as the slave owners of the south often called their slaves by classical Roman names.

The literature of the Hellenistic period, the time of the domination of the eastern Mediterranean, and further east, by the quarreling heirs of Alexander's generals, had a rich literary culture, including such poets as Callimachus and Apollonius Rhodius, and slaves figure prominently in it. The great poet Theokritos, a Sicilian who wrote in the court of the Ptolemies, writes of slaves in poetry that influenced the great Roman poet Vergil and the subsequent pastoral tradition, through the Renaissance Italians, to Milton and beyond. Herodas, writer of mimics, comic skits with affinities to Athenian Old Comedy, puts slaves at the centre of some of his works. His second mime is spoken by a brothel keeper, probably a eunuch, who keeps slave-prostitutes, and accuses a merchant of damaging his wares. He offers the woman for purchase, offers himself for torture, and shamelessly addresses the law court, pointing out the rips and tears in his prostitute's garments. In mime Five: 'The jealous woman accuses one of her slaves, whom she had made her favourite, of infidelity; has him bound and sent degraded through the town to receive two thousand lashes; no sooner is he out of sight than she recalls him to be tattooed "at one job."[16] In this comic sketch, the slave Gastron is subjected to violent threats and humiliation and is clearly vulnerable to the sexual predations of his free mistress. Slaves in the Hellenistic period may have been more cruelly and coercively treated than those of the classical period, or these mimes may simply be reflecting an elite view of lower class life. Still, the incidence of slave rebellion in the last two centuries BCE may indicate more difficult circumstances for slaves as the Romans move into new territory, sweeping up not only the Western Mediterranean, but also manipulating, intervening politically in, invading and eventually controlling the kingdoms once ruled by various descendants of Alexander's companions.

Slavery in Rome

Rome went quickly from a small hilltop village to a huge world power. It first overpowered and assimilated its Italian neighbours then went on to conquer nearby terrain, including the islands of the Western Mediterranean, site of Phoenician, that is, Carthaginian and Greek colonies, Spain and North Africa. It began conquest in the east by interfering with the monarchs of the Hellenistic kingdoms, subjected mainland Greece and continued expansion westward and eastward in a stunning drive toward hegemony over much of its known world. The empire was formed in the period of the Roman republic, and those who benefited from the immense increase in power, the ruling classes of Rome, dominated not just their own city but a vast territory beyond it. As Keith Bradley observes, in his important account of slave revolts in Rome:

> Incipient world rule . . . was the chief product of Roman military expansion in the middle Republic (264 BCE-146 BCE) But for the men and their families who comprised Rome's political elite, a further consequence was a rise in personal wealth on an enormous scale.[17]

In the transition to empire, Roman armies brought riches back to Italy, booty that was used by those already wealthy to increase their land-holdings. The army was manned by peasants taken from their farms, who sold their small parcels to the wealthy. And the peasants who had worked the land were replaced 'by the vast numbers of slaves thrown onto the market in the age of territorial expansion.' (19) War captives became domestic and agricultural slaves, owned by these wealthy Roman citizens, and the austere culture of farmer-soldier-statesmen was transformed forever, with consequences the Romans both celebrated and deplored, often seeing the contamination of Roman mores by floods of foreigners, slave and free, as a dangerous departure from the past.

Throughout the lands conquered or dominated by Roman power, especially in the transition from Hellenistic or Greek kingdoms to provinces of Rome, slaves seem to have been more exploited and oppressed than ever before, working in conditions of concentration previously unknown. Diodorus Siculus, for example, offers this portrait of the life of miners who worked in the mines of Egypt during the Ptolemaic period:

> No leniency or respite of any kind is given to any man who is sick, or maimed, or aged, or in the case of a woman for her weakness, but all without exception are compelled by blows to persevere in their labours, until through ill-treatment they die in the midst of their tortures.

The author observes that, in dread of an always worsening future, the miners look forward to death. With nothing to lose, such slaves were susceptible to revolutionary ideas. War captives were particularly unruly, having often grown to adulthood as free persons only to be captured and enslaved in circumstances of violence and terror. These slaves might be ex-soldiers themselves, trained in the use of weapons, unused to conditions of social death and dishonour and more liable to unite with others in the same circumstances, who shared their experiences, sometimes even their languages. Bradley calls 'the scale on which Rome enslaved prisoners of war' 'colossal.'

(21) and rebellions flared up in these populations. The historian Livy records slave rebellions in Setia and Praeneste and in Apulia, where there were many slave herdsmen. Of an episode of slave revolt in Etruria, the former land of the Etruscans, north of Rome, Livy chronicles these facts:

> . . . a slave conspiracy created a great danger in Etruria, Manius Acilius Glabrio, the praetor who exercised jurisdiction between citizens and foreigners, was dispatched with one of the two legions in the city to investigate and to repress the rebellion . . . . he defeated in battle others [slaves] who had already congregated in groups. Many of these were killed, and many others were taken prisoner. Some of the slaves, who were the leaders of the conspiracy, Glabrio ordered to be crucified after they had been whipped. Others he returned to their masters. (*History of Rome*, 33.36.1–3)[18]

Besides the revolts of the mine slaves at Laurion, mentioned earlier, and those at Delos, in the great slave depot there in the eastern Aegean, there were, before the Spartacus revolt, two Sicilian slave wars in the second century BCE. In Sicily, a factor supporting the revolt seems to have been the presence of many slaves who shared a common language, or who came from the Hellenized territories of Asia Minor. The leaders of these Sicilian slave wars had monarchic ambitions themselves, and sought to set themselves up in the style of Syrian kings, in Sicily. Eunus, a Syrian enslaved in the town of Enna, gathered an army of slaves and a few poor free men, fought and defeated several Roman generals and even issued coins in his name before he was defeated.

There was also a revolt in Asia Minor itself at the time of the transfer of power from a descendant of the conquering force of Alexander, who left Pergamon to the Romans in his will. This revolutionary struggle was led by the Pergamene Aristonikos, who offered freedom to slave followers and may have had utopian ambitions. There is speculation that he may have been inspired by utopian fantasies, in the guise of travel narratives, composed by Hellenistic authors, or by Stoic philosophical ideas. A former supporter of the populist Tiberius Gracchus, a Roman reformer defeated in his ambitions to aid the Roman people against the dominant ruling class, named Blossius, was said after Gracchus's death to have joined Aristonikos in Asia Minor. But Aristonikos's revolution eventually failed, and Pergamon, the wealthy kingdom once controlled by the family of the Attalids, fell into the hands of the Romans.

Prisoners of war, from all these theatres of combat, continued to swell the numbers of slaves sent back to Italy. The Romans of the imperial period had much greater numbers of slaves than the Greeks, often concentrated in the *latifundia*, plantation-like farms, and were conscious of the dangers presented by this massive population of potentially rebellious others. Preimperial Romans, writing of the management of farms and agricultural endeavours, presented their views on the proper disciplining of the groups of slaves who worked together on these farms, under overseers who were sometimes slaves themselves. One slaveowner who provides advice about agricultural slave management is Varro, author of *On Agriculture*, written in the first century BCE. He offers advice on the control of slave herdsmen who were prone to join slave rebellions, perhaps because of their nomadic ways and isolation. Varro counsels: 'The slaves who pasture the herd animals should be required to spend the whole day with the animals . . . All of the herdsmen should be under the charge of a master herdsman, who, preferably, should be older and more experienced than the other slaves, since the other slaves will be more willing to obey someone who is older and more experienced.' (trans., Shaw, 36; Varro 2.10.2) Cato, another great figure from the Roman past, in the second century BCE, similarly wrote a work *On Agriculture*, in which he describes, among other farming advice, the importance of the choice and management of the *vilicus*, the overseer who must keep the slaves in line.

The slaveowner Columella, who wrote a treatise on agriculture in the first century CE, participated actively in the supervision of his living tools, his property, his slaves. He chatted with the slaves on his farm in a more casual manner than he did with those who worked for him in the city. He required that his slave managers obey his wishes in relation to his slaves and not, for example, unchain slaves who had been fettered according to the master's orders. Slaves who are subject to many different supervisors are especially vulnerable to unjust treatment, and Columella expresses the fear that slaves so treated will be especially dangerous. He proposes that they receive adequate food and drink, tested by the master, and recalls that at times he himself has heard slave complaints about their treatment. He is especially concerned with breeding female slaves, and rewards those most productive with easier work or even with freedom for those who have four children. Such slaves increase his property and his wealth.

The slaves on these vast agricultural properties, which provided profit and increased wealth to the elite of Rome, because they lived in great numbers in proximity to one another, were subject to subversive ideas and tendencies to revolt, and so much of the advice concerning their management focuses on how to prevent dissatisfaction, conspiracies and open rebellion on their part. And in the urban setting too, in the great city of Rome, where there was also an increasing number of slaves, although not concentrated in huge barracks and working the land, there was fear of slave insurrection. The Stoic philosopher Seneca, tutor and adviser of the emperor Nero until he committed suicide when he fell from favour, wrote in his moral essay *On Mercy*, discussed in the previous chapter:

> A proposal was once made in the senate to distinguish slaves from free men by their dress; it then became apparent how great would be the impending danger if our slaves should begin to count our number. (*On Mercy* 1.24.1)

Elsewhere in the same essay, in a passage warning the emperor of the dangers of a failure of mercy, he recalls that 'the cruelty even of men in private station has been avenged by the hands of slaves despite their certain risk of crucifixion.' (1. 26. 1) A Roman proverb had it: 'however many slaves, so many enemies.'

Much of our evidence, however, concerning the presence of slaves in the everyday life of the Romans, demonstrates not fear of slave revolt, but rather an intimacy with slaves, a reliance on them, and in representations that have their origins in Greek literary texts, a grudging admiration for the ingenuity of slaves. The fourth-century BCE Greek playwright Menander, whose 'New' comedies differed greatly from those of Aristophanes, with a novel emphasis on family life, romance and domesticity managed by clever slaves, had its influence on Roman theatre.[19] A further factor that may have contributed to a change in the representation of slaves is the history of the second of the two great comic writers of Rome, Terence and Plautus. The first, Plautus, was probably born about 254 BCE, perhaps in Umbria north of Rome. He relies on Greek New Comedy, and frequently puts on stage, as far as we can tell from later, acting versions of his plays, slaves who talk back to their masters, manipulate fathers and sons, and create endings of their liking for the dramas in which they meddle. Kathleen McCarthy, in her excellent study of Plautus's comedies, in comparing them to blackface minstrel shows, concludes: 'both kinds of entertainments provided the soothing spectacle of slaves who were content in their servitude.'[20] 'The second function of such entertainments grows out of masters' enjoyment of this childlike quality with which they have endowed fictive slaves.' (212) She sees in these fictions 'the contradiction of mastery itself, that masters' desire to see slaves as carefree (and thus mask the compulsion required to maintain the system),' in contrast to 'their own experience of the hard work involved in keeping up mastery.' (213) Comedy is the occasion for the staging of this contradiction.

The other great Roman comic playwright, Terence, was said to have been a slave, born in Carthage, in North Africa at the beginning of the second century BCE. Later biographical accounts report that he was taken to Rome by a Roman senator, Terentius Lucanus, who eventually gave him his freedom. Suetonius, in his *Lives of the Poets*, records: 'He is described as being of average height, slight build, and dark complexion.' He wrote plays in the vein of those of Plautus, often using Greek models, relying on the examples of Menander. His *Andria*, for example, resembles Menander's play of the same name, and features a slave Davos, who advises the young hero, son of his master, effecting a happy ending and marriage for a couple in love. In this speech, he addresses the young Pamphilus, who has complained about his love life:

> As your slave, sir, it's my duty to work hand and foot, night and day, and risk my life if only I can be of service to you. If things don't always go according to plan, you only have to forgive me. My efforts may not be successful, sir, but I do my best. Of course if you like, you can think up something better yourself and get rid of me.[21]

Another play is named, in Greek, Heauton *timoroumenos*, 'the self-tormentor,' although the dialogue is of course in Latin, of a particularly rich and colloquial variety. And the clever, cunning slave, inherited from fourth-century Greek comedy, plays an important role in the plays of both these Roman dramatists.

William Fitzgerald interprets the representation of slaves in Roman drama not only as characters like those of everyday life, but even more as fictions allowing imaginative liberties on the part of the free Roman audience:

> Doubtless slaves at Rome did resist and manipulate their masters to the best of their ability, but Plautus's clever slaves are not just portraits, however exaggerated, of their resistance. These lovable tricksters in their imaginary Greek setting can be read, among other things, as fantasy projections of the free, not so much portraits of slaves as others through whom the free could play out their own agenda.[22]

Roman slaves provided a fertile ground for their masters' imaginations of subjugation, liberty and revolt. As Fitzgerald wonderfully puts it: 'The slave is as essential as an eye and as irritating and inconsequential as an itch, and this paradoxical form of intimacy results in a paradoxical response, just as the hand that rubs the eye only aggravates the symptoms it is trying to alleviate.' (24) In scenes that descend genealogically from the intimate play between Xanthias and the god Dionysos in Aristophanes's *Frogs*, Roman comic playwrights depict new forms of identification, mirroring, and fantasy involving masters and their human possessions.

In love elegy, an important genre of Roman poetry, poets used the metaphor of slavery to describe their bondage to a beloved. Kathleen McCarthy cites Ovid, and, in a subtle and persuasive analysis of the play between poet, slave and beloved in Roman love elegy, reflects on what is at stake:

> The lover-as-slave in elegy ... employs to his advantage a vision of slaves already present in the anxieties of Roman mastery: a vision of the slave as someone who undermines, rather than assaults, who achieves control by a show of obedience and selflessness rather than by claiming authority outright. Thus the lover of elegy can deflect attention from his motives, under the cover of servile objectification, while the poet of elegy maintains an ironic distance from the degraded slave, and signals his control of the fictive situation by never allowing the slave's underhanded attempt to succeed.[23]

It may be that more frequent manumission, and the presence of many freedmen, former slaves now freed, with obligations still to their former masters, produced a radically different relationship between Roman slave-owners and their slaves, than that between Greeks and their slaves. Many more Roman slaves than Greek achieved freedom, buying their way out of slavery, freed by their masters and mistresses, living or dead. The poet Horace's father was a freedman, for example. 'Freedmen' constituted an important and sometimes powerful and wealthy class in Rome, even though the manumitted were bound by certain legal obligations to their former owners.

The Romans seem at times more conscious of feelings of intimacy with their slave companions, conscious of slaves' shared humanity with the free, and sometimes express more empathy with the condition of enslavement, even as their institutions of plantation agriculture, slavery used in their fleets and in mining, inflicted great brutality. The famed orator Cicero, for example, wrote letters to his favourite slave Tiro, his secretary who would be manumitted in 53 BCE: 'Indeed I want you to join me, but I am afraid of the journey . . . You must get ready to restore your services to my Muses. My promise will be performed on the appointed day (I have taught you the derivation of 'faith.') Now mind you get thoroughly well.' (Cicero to Tiro, Cumae, 17 April 53)[24] In this later letter Cicero again expresses concern for his freedman's health:

> One thing, my dear Tiro, I do beg of you: don't consider money at all when the needs of your health are concerned. I have told Curius to advance whatever you say , , , Your services to me are beyond count – in my home and out of it, in Rome and abroad, in private affairs and public, in my studies and literary work. You will cap them all if I see you your own man again, as I hope I shall. (Leucas, 7 November 50)

Cicero relied on Tiro throughout his career as a politician and orator, and, after his death, his freed slave served as a sort of literary executor, labouring in his master's name.

As noted earlier, the Romans freed far more slaves than did the Greeks. In his *Conquerors and Slaves* Keith Hopkins addresses this phenomenon, arguing that such practices suggest not a growing humanitarianism, but a strategy for sustaining the institution of slavery and for enriching the free:

> If we consider slavery as a system, then the liberation of slaves, whatever blessings it brought to individuals, acted not as a solvent of the slave system but as a major reinforcement. Emancipation reinforced slavery as a system because Roman slaves, frequently, even customarily in my view, paid substantial sums for their freedom. The prospect of becoming free kept a slave under control and hard at work, while the exaction of a market price as the cost of liberty enabled the master to buy a younger replacement. Humanity was complemented by self-interest.[25]

Even the moments of concern for their slaves, expressed by masters, must be seen in the light of the fundamental relationship of coercion, social death and dishonour implicit in all slavery.

The freedman's son Horace, in a poem that looks forward to a scene from the film Spartacus, rejoices in a simple domestic scene that includes a slave favourite:

> I scorn these Persian preciosities, boy—
> wreaths bound with linden bark, indeed,
> and inquiries as to where the last rose
>   is blowing.
>
> It is misplaced zeal to elaborate
> on simple myrtle. Here under trellised vines
> myrtle is correct both for me drinking,
>   you pouring.
>   (Odes 1.38)[26]

Although his own father had been a slave, Horace takes for granted his pleasure in the company of this boy, his possession.

The imperial families that ruled Rome and its extended territories at the height of Roman power, held many slaves. In a study of the emperor's freedmen and slaves, *Familia Caesaris*, P.R.C. Weaver describes the great extent of the imperial household, which stretched throughout the empire, and contained huge numbers of slaves and ex-slaves over centuries.[27]

> It comprised . . . the slaves that belonged to or came into the posses-
> sion of successive emperors either as personal property by family
> inheritance, private bequest, gift or by purchase, or as part of the
> *patrimonium* which passed from each emperor to his successor by
> virtue of his official position . . . The basic relationship between the
> ordinary *Caesaris servus* and the emperor, while it was essentially the
> legal one between master and slave, was complicated by the great size

and geographical diffusion of the Familia Caesaris throughout the empire. (4)

There were great opportunities for advancement in the Caesars' households, for clever and useful slaves, and a hierarchy that developed among different orders of slaves and between the still-enslaved and the freed persons who remained attached to the imperial house.

In the scandalous *Lives of the Caesars*, gossipy, lurid and sensational, slaves figure variously in the careers of the members of the imperial house. Suetonius recounts this adventure in the life of Nero:

> Having tried to turn the boy Sporus into a girl by castration, he went through a wedding ceremony with him – dowry, bridal veil and all – which the whole Court attended; then brought him home, and treated him as a wife. He dressed Sporus in the fine clothes normally worn by an Empress and took him in his own litter not only to every Greek assize and fair, but actually through the Street of Images at Rome, kissing him amorously now and then. (Life of Nero, 28)[28]

Not content with playing the role of bridegroom to Sporus, Nero later takes on the role of bride: his freedman 'Doryphorus now married him – just as he himself had married Sporus – and on the wedding night he imitated the screams and moans of a girl being deflowered.' (29)

The imperial period evinced much cruelty, toward slaves as well as citizens, on the part of emperors, senatorial class slaveowners and even by slaves themselves who owned slaves. The satirist Juvenal, who wrote during the first two centuries of the common era, mockingly records many episodes of deliberate or incidental cruelty, with indignation, although he never challenges the institution of slavery itself. 'Is it not plain lunacy/To lose ten thousand on a turn of the dice, yet grudge/A shirt to your shivering slave?' (Satire 1)[29] Some of his scorn is directed at former slaves, recently freed, who do not know their place. Satire VI, directed against women, in the misogynist tradition of the Greek Hesiod and Semonides, indicts women for their sadism toward slaves, forcing masters against their will to abuse their power:

'Crucify that slave!'

                    'But what is the slave's offence
To merit such punishment? Who has brought charges against him?
Where are the witnesses? You must hear his defence: no
Delay can be too long when a man's life is at stake.'
'So a slave's a *man*, now, is he, you crackpot? All right, perhaps
He didn't do anything. This is still my wish, my command:
Warrant enough that I will it.' (Satire 6, p.135)

The epigrammatist Martial, a contemporary of Juvenal records similar impulses in a man he calls Ponticus:

> Why did you cut out your slave's tongue,
> Ponticus, and then have him hung
> Crucified? Don't you realize, man,
> Though he can't speak, the rest of us can? (2.82)[30]

Although he, like Martial, condemns excessive cruelty, Juvenal's sympathy rarely extends to slaves unless he is using violence used against them to satirize another target. The wife neglected in bed by her husband takes out her rage on her slaves, with beatings, whippings, floggings: 'Some women pay their floggers an annual salary.' (145) 'The slave-girl/Arranging her coiffure will have her own hair torn out.' (146) Rutilus, object of one of the satires, is accused of indiscriminate joy in beating slaves as well, in a formulation that, like Aristotle's long before, hints at arguments circulating concerning the natural equality of slaves:

> Does he hold that slaves are fashioned, body and soul, from the same
> Elements as their masters? Not on your life. What he teaches
> Is sadism, pure and simple: there's nothing pleases him more
> Than a good old noisy flogging, no siren song to compare

With the crack of the lash. To his quaking household he's
A monster, a mythical ogre, never so happy as when
The torturer's there on the job, and some poor wretch who's stolen
A couple of towels is being branded with red-hot irons.

(Satire XIV, p, 263)

Like the slaves of ancient Babylonia, Rutilus's slaves are marked with their
master's brand. This slave owner is satirized for his perverse delight in chains,
dungeons, burnt flesh and labour camps the *ergastula*, buried dormitories
in which the field-slaves were held and from which, on the advice of such
agricultural experts as Cato, they were turned out when they were too old
to work. Slaves who lived in houses like Rutilus's, when one of their number
murdered the master, were all put to death, however many, however innocent, as a deterrent to other such murderous impulses, as an example to
other households and to encourage slaves to reveal any conspiracies brewing
against their masters.

In another mood, pointing to the hidden transcripts, always suspected
in a society with such profound differences of status, Juvenal claims that
the only reason to lead a honourable life is to protect oneself from a slave's
gossip: 'First among many reasons for decent living, surely,/Is the need to
be proof against the malice of your slaves:/ The tongue is a slave's worse
part.' (9, p. 199)

In another epigram, Martial refers to the slave-market, the vulnerability
of any person owned by another to be sold. He uses the occasion to mock
the seller; the slave prostitute is seen with contempt, contaminated further
by the broker's dirty mouth:

Last week, the auctioneer was trying to sell
A girl whose reputation one could smell
From here to her street corner in the slums.
After some time, when only paltry sums
Were being offered, wishing to assure
The crowd that she was absolutely pure,

He pulled the unwilling 'lot' across and smacked
Three or four kisses on her. Did this act
Make any difference to the price? It did.
The highest offerer withdrew his bid. (6.66)

The ugliness of the scene is enhanced by the epigrammatist's disgust at the prostitute's impurity; like the brother owner of Herodas's first mime, this broker displays the goods on offer, the woman's body, all that she has for sale, and then further damages her with his sexual attentions. The outrage felt by abolitionists at such scenes in the antebellum period in the US is inconceivable here; Martial feels sympathy neither for the prostitute nor for her seller. In other poems he praises and consigns to death his barber (6.52), and the little girl with a Greek name, like many others, Erotion, just five years old: 'the slave I loved,' whom he tenderly sends on to his parents in the underworld, so that she will not there be frightened. He asks that the earth not lie heavy on her: 'She put so little weight on you.' (5.34) Such extremes of disgust at some of the enslaved, and tenderness in relation to domestic slaves, who lived in such intimate surroundings, often, with their masters, characterize the complexities of relations between slave and free in the Roman world. Although there is no call for abolition, there is ambivalence, slaves who were ridiculed, slaves who were beloved.

The later Stoic emperor Marcus Aurelius, in his *Meditations*, reminds himself that anyone can lose his serenity and equilibrium when enslaved, an attitude that might have resulted in a more sober and respectful attitude toward his slaves, consistent with the Stoic teaching that one's place in the hierarchy of statuses meant nothing, but rather that the good, virtuous, philosophical man would conduct himself properly, as emperor or slave. Such attitudes in the philosophical schools, the cultivation of indifference to status, to pain and suffering and an acceptance of one's place in the universe without complaint, contributed to the Christians' attitudes toward enslavement, their acceptance of the institution of slavery, as noted in the previous chapter, in the letters of Paul, for example, and in the embrace of the metaphor of slavery as a characterization of the proper relationship of the believer to his or her god.

The Christian Augustine, a man of the old pagan world, as well as a figure of transition to a new, Christian Europe, had this to say, in a formulation that demonstrates his reliance not only on the customary practices of the pagan Greeks and Romans, but also on the legacy of the Hebrew Bible and the Christian New Testament: 'The prime cause of slavery is sin, so that man was put under man in a state of bondage; and this can be only by a judgement of God, in whom there is no unrighteousness, and who knows how to assign divers punishments according to the deserts of the sinners.'[31] As Peter Garnsey points out, Augustine builds on the thinking of his Christian predecessor, Paul, the Jewish Philo, and his superior Ambrose, and recognizes the justice of the slavery all around him, which was a feature especially of war and captivity in the pagan domain:

> Augustine's account of slavery of man to man takes in all slavery in a second sense: not just the Old Testament enslavements, but also the standard wartime enslavements of his world and preceding periods of history and, in general, enslavement through adversity or misfortune. Sin lay behind all of these enslavements. (219)

This is the legacy passed on to the Christian tradition, in a synthesis of Aristotle's natural slavery with the enslavement to god of the Israelites and the acceptance of and resignation to slavery of the earliest Christians. Such views lead not to calls for abolition, but rather to indifference to the worldly condition of slavery, a supposed indifference to one's status in the earthly realm that precedes eternity and a recognition of original sin, the sin of Adam and Eve that led all human beings to live in bondage.

CHAPTER V

SPARTACUS AND *GLADIATOR*: SLAVES IN FILM

One of the stranger legacies of the long history of legal slavery in Western civilization is a manifestation of the twenty-first century, so-called 'plantation tourism,' or 'dark tourism,' or 'thanatourism.'[1] The developing industry for tourists visiting Auschwitz, the slave plantations of the Caribbean and slave markets in Ghana and the southern states of the US, represents a disturbing yet necessary dimension of the present's coming to terms with the past. The sanitizing and misrepresentations at some of these sites bespeak the insistent drive to render the story of Western civilization as one of unending progress, yet there is also a recognition of an unconscious, a darker side of the history of the West, a curiosity about the beginnings of racialised slavery, for example, or about the culmination of millennia of anti-Semitism in the death camps of Nazi Germany.

Students of tourism point to the ways in which such tourism can produce a falsified image of the past, dubbed by one scholar 'distory,'[2]; the tourism industry in the Caribbean:

> . . . has been quick to realize that it cannot portray its history as it really happened, since the presentation of centuries of overt racism, slavery, cruelty, bloodshed and exploitation, with all the corresponding guilt that it could evoke in the descendants of the perpetrators, is hardly a recipe for touristic success. There has consequently been a selective rendition of the past based on collective amnesia . . . .[3]

Tourism in Barbados offers a nostalgic trip into the past for those who want to imagine themselves in the role of planters; they are provided with luxury accommodations in plantation houses, so-called 'dinner-shows,' that claim to reproduce life on the plantations as slave processions into the fields, and dances of 'emancipation.' (68) Of course, the economies of these sites can become dependent on such tourism, and the descendants of racialised slaves employed to represent their ancestors in a new simulacrum of slavery; the ironies multiply. Rey Chow writes, 'where have all the natives gone?' Historians of slavery may crave authenticity, a more historical, respectful attitude toward these histories of slavery, but the inhabitants of the present world system may have other ideas. Patience Essah describes the tourism industry developing in Ghana, once the Gold Coast, and cites 'Ghana's continuing interest in drawing tourists from all over the world, especially among Africans of the diaspora, to the nation's monuments to slavery and the slave trade.'[4] Touristic sites related to the history of slavery include the slave labour and death camps of the Nazis, other forts and slave-loading ports of Western Africa, as well as the plantations, slave quarters and slave markets of the American South. Such destinations are subject to white-washing and manipulation, comforting those who seek pleasure in a past where they imagine themselves as masters, but they can not only provide income to poor nations of the global south, but also remind visitors of the economic arrangements of the past that led to the inequalities of the present. And, in some cases, they can even point to possibilities of struggle against domination, and conflict that led to emancipation for the slaves of the past, like the Haitian revolutionaries led by Toussaint Louverture. Rather than the Disneyfication, the sanitizing of episodes of genocide, slavery and exploitation of the past, these sites can remind visitors of suffering and of heroic resistance against suffering. A coming to terms with the past occurs not only in such tourism, in visiting the sites of episodes from the troubled past, but also in excursions into the past like the reading of historical novels and viewing other works of art that depict historical events. In this chapter I consider some cinematic versions of the history of the West, in films made in the twentieth century: the enslavement and liberation of the

Hebrew slaves in Pharaonic Egypt, a part of the probably imaginary epic past of Israel, the slave revolt of the first century BCE led by the slave and gladiator Spartacus, and the fictional account of Maximus, general, slave, gladiator, in the film *Gladiator*.

Like the thanatourism of the present day, these films visit imaginatively sites of the past, in this case the sites of ancient slavery. They acknowledge, unlike some other cultural representations of antiquity, the fact of ancient slavery. Museums, for instance, often suppress the presence of slaves in the everyday life of ancient people, leaving out the omnipresence of slaves in scenes represented on works of art, slaves' roles in the production of those very works of art and in all the sites of ancient life. The figuring of slavery in historical film, however, is a special case; the fictions centered on ancient slavery have allegorical power. Ancient slaves speak to modern audiences because of messages they convey not only about beginnings, about origins, of their communities, but also about the enabling ideologies of the nations that produce the films. Since the enlightenment, since abolitionist movements of the modern period, since human rights efforts of the twentieth century, the identification of the cinema audience, unlike that of the audience of Roman poetry, for example, is led toward the slaves rather than the masters. Even though there is ambiguity, a complexity in the viewers' reading of cinematic fictions, one that allows for split identifications, a nostalgia for mastery, for example, in the case of slavery, the explicit thrust of the film-maker's art is usually a condemnation of the institution of slavery, and a heroizing of the resistant slave, or slaves.

In his work on cinema, the French philosopher Gilles Deleuze, who wrote about the historical films of the earlier twentieth century, usefully characterized the work of D.W. Griffith and Cecil B. De Mille, who made an earlier *Ten Commandments* in 1923, before the Technicolour version of 1956, to be discussed below, starring Charlton Heston as Moses.

> ... the American cinema constantly shoots and reshoots a single fundamental film, which is the birth of a nation-civilisation, whose first version was provided by Griffith.[5]

Deleuze here refers to D.W. Griffith's film *Birth of a Nation*, released in 1915, which recounts the history of the Civil War in the United States, the impact on north and south and the foundation of the Ku Klux Klan, the murderously racist group organized after the abolition of slavery to maintain white supremacy in the southern United States.

Deleuze points to the narcissism of American cinema: 'it and it alone is the whole of history, the germinating stock from which each nation-civilisation detaches itself as an organism, each prefiguring America.' (149) He points out that, as in the 1923 version of *The Ten Commandments*, which featured a parallelism between the ancient world and the United States, the 'decadent nations are sick organisms.'

> If the Bible is fundamental to them, it is because the Hebrews, then the Christians, gave birth to healthy nation-civilisations which already displayed the two characteristics of the American dream: that of a melting pot in which minorities are dissolved and that of a ferment which creates leaders capable of reacting to all situations. (149)

Deleuze draws the parallel between John Ford's young Mr. (Abraham) Lincoln and Cecil B. De Mille's Moses, both of whom negotiate a transition from 'the nomadic to the written law.' The foundation of the United States was a belated event, from the point of view of this Parisian, and American film therefore treats all genres to some degree as 'historical.' Biblical and toga epics, Westerns and gangster movies, all look to a past that is fictionalised and treated as a myth of origin.

Deleuze also cites the nineteenth-century German philosopher Friedrich Nietzsche, who distinguished among three different aspects of history, the monumental, the antiquarian, and the critical or ethical. Deleuze describes the early historical epics, the American films that look back to Egypt, Babylon and Rome, as 'monumental,' dwelling on 'the natural and archi-tectural milieu.' (149) In fact, the monumental aspect of the historical epics is not confined to the early twentieth century; the computer-generated images of the late twentieth and early twenty-first century films representing antiquity similarly rejoice in the broad sweep, the great encompassing vast-nesses of fleets at sea, and cheering or jeering crowds in the Colosseum.

Deleuze makes the point that, following Nietzsche's analysis of the 'monu-mental' in history, this aspect of history:

> favours the analogies or parallels between one civilization and another: the great moments of humanity, however distant they are, are supposed to communicate via the peaks, and form a 'collection of effects in themselves' which can be more easily compared and act all the more strongly on the mind of the modern spectator. Monumental history thus naturally tends toward the universal. (149)

In the films discussed in this chapter, the filmmakers assume a hatred of slavery, a desire for freedom and an identification with the heroic slaves that is universalized. The situation in these ancient settings is allegorized to encompass what the American directors assume is a natural hunger for freedom and escape from bondage, a naturalization that echoes American ideas about the foundation of the nation, even though the nation was in fact built on the genocide of indigenous people and the enslavement of Africans. The myth of escape from oppression, the 'huddled masses yearning to be free,' from Emma Lazarus's poem, inscribed on the Statue of Liberty, informs profoundly these accounts of antiquity on film.

The Ten Commandments

If we consider the history, and the impact in Western political theory of episodes of resistance to slavery, one of the most powerful inherited models is the divinely sanctioned rebellion of the Hebrew slaves of ancient Egypt against their masters, which led to their liberation and the conquest of the land of the Canaanites, mentioned in Chapter Three. This is of course a highly compromised story, believed now by archaeologists to be a retro-spectively imagined fiction that establishes an ideology of persecution and escape for the people who came to consider themselves Israelites, and used as a justification for conquest of others' land not only by the modern Zionist movement, but also by North Americans, South Africans and others. It has also served, however, as an account inspiring hope and insurrection among slave communities in modernity, in the African diaspora, for example, in the Rastafarian community.

The story of the Israelites and their escape from captivity in Egypt figures not only in the Hebrew Bible, but also in films in the twentieth century. *The Ten Commandments*, made by Cecil B. De Mille first in 1923, and then re-produced in 1956 and starring Charlton Heston as Moses, represents the struggle of the slaves of the Pharaoh, played in the later version by Yul Brynner, in a memorable and spectacular set of scenes celebrating the liberation of a captive people. The 1923 version of De Mille's epic begins with a direct reference to the 'World War,' so recently ended, and declares firmly that the ten commandments offer 'a way out.' The Ten Commandments are not laws but 'the Law.' The first part of this silent film covers the story of Exodus, using the Hebrew Bible for its written texts, which are interspersed with scenes taken from the Bible, and filmed on a huge set built on a sandy beach in Southern California that represents ancient Egypt. De Mille recalls the bitterness of the First World War, and connects it with the bitterness of the Israelite slaves' bondage to the Egyptians. The monumentality of the sets confirms Deleuze's categorization of this epic; De Mille begins with an immense Egyptian head, then shows the cruel overseer flogging the labouring slaves as they haul a huge sphinx. The slaves are denied rest, and we see the anguish of Miriam, Moses's sister.

Throughout these sequences, the filmmaker uses the immensity of Pharaonic spaces to great effect. The stiff hieratic postures of silent film seem perfect for the formality and pageantry of the Egyptian court; the viewer encounters the sterility of the Oriental, replete with smoking altars, and the scarab face of the Pharaoh's god, who cannot restore life after his son is struck down in the tenth and last of the plagues sent by the Hebrews' god. The fabulous settings, and the ornate, art deco costuming of Egyptians, establishes a difference, a barbarism in the slaveholders, who are challenged by the bearded, robed patriarch of the Israelites. After the boy's death, Pharoah sends the Israelites away, and they depart like war refugees from between the wings of the vast palace, the way lined with sphinxes. The pursuit by the Egyptian charioteers, led by Rameses, is thwarted by a wall of fire, and the Israelites pass between two immense walls of water that then swallow up the pursuing army. Moses on Mount Sinai receives the commandments, but the former slaves fall into dissolution, stroking and worshipping a phallic gold calf, in scenes that foreshadow the errors of the present day. There is voluptuous, lascivious writhing about, kissing, fondling, even rope dancing, but the erstwhile queen of the decadent celebrations suddenly becomes a leper! Moses returns, and the golden calf is smashed.

Abruptly, De Mille segues to a bible reading in a twentieth-century family and the rest of the film, which never returns to the scenes of the Hebrew Bible, describes the fate of those who fail to obey the ten commandments written in light on the screen in the earlier scenes, transcribed by Moses on the tablets, and then smashed to the ground when Moses sees the corruption of his people. In the modern scenes, one of Mrs. McTavish's sons reveals his atheism, breaks every commandment, through his negligence even killing his own mother. He steals his brother's sweetheart, she herself an atheist, blaspheming thief. The most exciting commandment, forbidding adultery, involves 'a half-Chinese, half-French seductress,' named 'Sally Lung.' This plot strand wallows in orientalism.

Although the narrator's voice, as Dan McTavish sinks into depravity, intones: 'If you break the Ten Commandments they will break you,' he must break every commandment. And in a recapitulation of the golden calf episode, we learn that Sally Lung is an escapee from the leper colony on Molokai. She is killed; McTavish's life is destroyed, as he breaks the last of the commandments. His once-defiant and depraved wife seeks out her former beau, a carpenter, and led by him she finds Jesus, who cures her of leprosy, in a dream-like, historical flashback in which the New Testament enters the plot. Jesus says: 'Be thou made clean,' and her leprosy is gone! The theme of leprosy touches on fears of venereal disease, racism in relation to Asian immigrants and demands for quarantine, and has its parallels in cinematic versions of the novel *Ben Hur*, in which Jesus cures the mother and sister of the hero of leprosy.

The matter of slavery, in this first of De Mille's *Ten Commandments*, appears in the first sequence, in the sufferings and debasement of the Hebrews at the hands of the Egyptians. Nothing alludes to the enslavement of the Israelites to their god, to their law, to one another; nor is there any reference to the recent history of mass racialised slavery in nineteenth-century America, so important to the work of D.W. Griffith. In De Mille's silent movie, the enslavement is overcome, nothing is made of the early biography of Moses, and the emphasis is on establishing the Law, a Law which, in De Mille's view, must still be obeyed in the twentieth century, if his viewers are to find 'a way out' of the bitterness and despair produced by the ravages of the first world war.

Cecil B. De Mille's second version of *The Ten Commandments*, released almost thirty-five years later, in 1956, came in the wake of another 'world' war, the holocaust of the European Jews and the foundation of the state of Israel after a violent civil war led by Jewish terrorists such as Yitzhak Rabin. These events haunt the new version of *The Ten Commandments*. After the musical overture, a man emerges from behind a curtain, acknowledging that this is an unusual procedure, but that this is an unusual subject. This is 'the story of the birth of freedom,' the story of Moses. He notes that the Hebrew Bible 'omits' the early life of Moses, up until the moment he 'learned he was Hebrew,' so the film-makers relied on Philo and Josephus. The master-of-ceremonies announces that: The theme of this 'picture' is whether men are to be ruled by God's law, or the whims of a dictator like Rameses. And he underlines the allegorical, contemporary significance of this theme by adding: 'This same battle continues throughout the world today,' in a reference to the cold war between the US and its allies and the Soviet Union and its allies, always characterized as a dictatorship, a tyranny, by Western governments. These remarks are made in the midst of the anti-Communist, red-baiting, McCarthyist days of the Eisenhower presidency. The solemnity and gravity of the occasion are stressed, many academic experts thanked, scholars from the Metropolitan Museum, the University of Chicago, the

Jewish Library of Los Angeles, and the preview announces that those who view this movie make 'a pilgrimage over the very ground that Moses trod,' as it cites Philo, Josephus, Eusebius, the Midrash and the Holy Scriptures. After this portentous prelude, the film proper begins with creation and then, suddenly, 'freedom was gone from the world,' and we see a huge statue of Pharaoh pulled by lines of slaves, and a new-born baby, Moses, the 'one man to stand alone against an empire.' The narrative focuses on the biography of this one man, the heroic, compassionate, athletic individual who will save the world and deliver his people from their enslavement.

We first see the grown-up Moses, played by Charlton Heston, as he rides in triumph celebrating his victory over the Ethiopians. Moses shows mercy and respect toward these Africans, as he announces to his adoptive father, the Pharaoh Sethi, 'Great one, I bring you Ethiopia,' in friendship, as an ally. Moses is 'kind as well as wise,' says the Ethiopian princess, and the Ethiopians, in extravagant feathered costumes, dance spectacularly for the Pharaoh, throwing tribute at his feet. The booty is destined for the new 'treasure city', which has stalled in its construction, because the Hebrew slaves believe a 'deliverer' has come to free them. The princely Moses is delegated to build the city; Rameses sends to find the deliverer and have him brought, if he exists, in chains. At the construction site in Goshen, the slaves, thirsty, oppressed, are driven mercilessly; 'is life in bondage better than death?' asks Joshua.

These scenes of the film allude to the atmosphere of the Nazi death camps, with its starving hordes of slaves, and Dathan, the cruel chief Hebrew overseer played by Edward G. Robinson, resembles the 'kapo,' one of the Jewish overseers in the slave labour camps who bought their own lives by working for the Nazis. A Hebrew woman, caught under one of the immense stones of the growing treasure city, is about to be crushed to death, but Moses, supervising the labour, spares her, showing an innate mercy and saying: 'Blood makes poor mortar.'

The natural nobility and goodness of the Hebrew Moses, even though he himself and all around him believe him to be an Egyptian prince, reveal themselves in such acts of mercy. The dialogue revels in such lines as these:

'You do not speak like a slave.' 'God made men; men made slaves.' 'It is not treason to want freedom.' Moses feeds the slaves, opening the priests' granaries, and gives them one day in seven to rest. The princess Nefretiri learns of his slave origins, and kills the slave, not one of the Hebrews, who reveals them. This slave had warned Moses's adoptive mother against her taking him from the basket in the bulrushes, and she tries to convince Nefretiri not to ally herself with the blood of the despised Hebrews. Her situation as a slave and her murder are incidental to the plot; she is not one of the chosen people. Then Moses himself learns of his slave birth, gives up his position as the potential heir of the Pharaoh, and suitor to his daughter, and accepts leadership of the Hebrew slaves, who labour in terrible suffering. Moses joins them. The environment of the Nazi slave labour camps is evoked again in the emaciation of the slaves, their abjection, the humiliation and degradation of the Hebrew women. Like Spartacus, an old man defiantly says, 'We are not animals.'

Much of this early section of the film dwells on the issue of 'passing,' living in disguise, the term used to describe gay men and women who live passing as heterosexuals, or as in the novel of Nella Larsen, *Passing*, living in white society as white, while having grown up in an African-American world. In this case, Moses was incognito, passing as a 'Gentile,' his role implicitly critiquing a denial of one's Jewish identity, perhaps in some allusion to the situation of the Jews in Germany before the rule of the Nazis, or to those assimilated in American culture, who have forgotten or deny their Jewish roots. In some sense, like the later film *Exodus*, the film serves as a call to remind Jews of their identity, a call back to orthodoxy, or to support of the nascent nation of Israel.

Moses, for killing a sexual predator, the master builder played by an effete Vincent Price, ends up in chains before the Pharaoh, and is condemned; he travels across the desert to the sheikhdom of Midian, where he marries and has a son. When Joshua reminds him of the suffering of the Hebrew slaves back in Egypt, Moses goes up the mountain, sees the burning bush and asks why the god neglects his people, in slavery. The god says that after Moses brings them out of Egypt, 'They shall serve *me*.' After the ten plagues, and the killing of the first-born of the Egyptians, the Hebrew slaves are allowed to depart. 'A nation arose, and freedom was born into the world,' says the voice-over, and Moses leads them out of bondage, in a scene that echoes the first *Ten Commandments*, a great mass of freed slaves, this time filmed in glorious colour, that passes between the lines of sphinxes. Only the cruel, predatory and traitorous Dathan, the slave who became more of an oppressor than the slaveowners themselves, wants to stay behind. Again, Moses parts the sea until the new nation has passed; the walls of water come down on the Egyptians, and only Rameses is spared, Rameses who finally admits to Anne Baxter (the Eve of *All About Eve*), 'His god *is* god.' Moses's last words are: 'Go, proclaim liberty to all the lands, unto all the inhabitants thereof.' Liberty, the slogan of the French Revolution, becomes the call of the mid-century American empire and of the conquerors-to-be of the land of milk and honey.

The representation of Israelite society, in its enslavement to the Egyptians, in its escape from the Pharaoh and his army, in its wandering in the desert, does not acknowledge the presence of slaves within it in the promised land itself. As made clear in Chapter Three, the Hebrew Bible accepts and regulates not only the enslavement of Israelites by one another, but also the possession of slaves from other peoples. Perhaps the blindness to these slaves, their erasure from the immense canvas of De Mille's epic, owes much to the post-civil war horror of slavery; but it bodes ill for the relationship between the Israelites, the Israelis, ancient and modern, who came to live among peoples with beliefs different from their own, Canaanites and Palestinian Christians and Muslims. The great emphasis on liberation from bondage, deliverance from slavery, and arrival in the promised land, cannot include a recognition of the historical fact of continued slavery among the people of the Hebrew Bible. The metaphor of slavery, of redemption by the god and a kind of sale, possession and obligation that persists beyond the wandering in the desert, does not figure in the representation of these events in De Mille's epic. The conquest of Canaan, and the enslavement of the indigenous peoples, have their legacy in the tormented relationship of the Palestinians to the Israelis and of the Muslim Israelis to their Jewish fellow citizens in modern Israel.

Spartacus

The movie *Spartacus*, released in 1960 and starring Kirk Douglas, is the only one of these movies based on historical facts as recorded in Roman texts, those of various ancient historians, including Livy, Plutarch, Sallust, Appian and Florus. According to Plutarch, who gives a continuous version of the story in his *Life of Crassus*, Spartacus, a Thracian slave, was among a group of gladiators being trained in the southern Italian city of Capua. Several hundred of them, unwilling to be forced into gladiatorial combats in which they would eventually be killed, planned their escape from the camp. Their plan was betrayed, but, nonetheless, seventy-two of them grabbed kitchen knives and skewers and forced their way out. On the road outside, they came across some wagons carrying weapons for gladiators in another city, which they seized. Armed, they chose three leaders, with Spartacus as chief. Plutarch adds that he was from a nomadic Thracian tribe, 'more of a Greek than the people of his country usually are.'[6] Then the gladiators defeated the Capuans . . . who came out against them, and took their weapons. Clodius, the Roman praetor, brought three thousand men from Rome, and besieged them but they swung down from their mountain refuge on wild vines and encircled the Romans from behind. Shepherds and herdsmen, always likely suspects to join revolts, came over to their side. More Romans were sent to oppose them, and more were routed. Spartacus almost captured another Roman, Cossinius, at Salinae, where he was bathing, took his camp and killed Cossinius.

Spartacus then marched his growing army toward the Alps, planning to cross them and send his men back to their homelands in Gaul or Thrace. But they preferred to ravage Italy and continued to defeat those Roman forces sent against them. Finally the Senate took over from the consuls, and appointed Crassus, subject of Plutarch's *Life*, as general in charge of defeating Spartacus, and 'a great many of the nobility went volunteers with him, partly out of friendship, and partly to get honour.' (656) At first Crassus's lieutenant Mummius, with two legions, engaged against orders with the rebels and was routed, while the soldiers, fleeing, lost their weapons.

> Crassus rebuked Mummius, and, arming the soldiers again, he made them find sureties for their arms . . . and five hundred that were the beginners of the flight he divided into fifty tens, and one of each was to die by lot, thus reviving the ancient Roman punishment of decimation, where ignominy is added to the penalty of death, with a variety of appalling and terrible circumstances, presented before the eyes of the whole army, assembled as spectators. (656)

This theatre of cruelty had its effect, and the army marched again against Spartacus's forces. Spartacus then tried to reach Sicily, striking a deal with some Cilician pirates. He thought he could connect with the Sicilian rebels who had fought two earlier slave wars, one of which was 'but lately extinguished, and seemed to need but little fuel to set it burning again.' But the pirates betrayed him, took his money and sailed away.

Spartacus set up the army at the peninsula of Rhegium, now Reggio di Calabria, and Crassus decided to fence him in there, with a wall and a ditch across the isthmus. Spartacus managed to fill up the ditch with dirt and tree boughs, and took a third of his army across back into Italy. Crassus feared that he was about to march on Rome itself. But, after some Roman success, Crassus began to regret that he had asked for other Roman generals to join him, since he wanted credit for defeating Spartacus himself. He tried to attack secretly some mutineers who had left the main body of Spartacus's army, but the troops were discovered by 'two women who were sacrificing for the enemy.' There was a great battle, in which the rebels fought heroically: 'Of twelve thousand three hundred whom he killed, two only were found wounded in their backs, the rest all having died standing in their ranks and fighting bravely.' (657)

The slaves, encouraged by their victories, refused now to avoid confrontation with the enemy, and they turned back toward Crassus. He was eager to win victory before his rival Pompey arrived. Spartacus saw that he could not avoid a battle and 'when his horse was brought him, he drew out his sword and killed him, saying, if he got the day he should have a great many better horses of the enemies', and if he lost it he should have no need of this.' (658) He charged directly at Crassus, missed him, but killed two centurions. Then, surrounded by the enemy, he stood his ground, as Plutarch acknowledges, 'bravely defending himself', and was cut in pieces. After the defeat, Pompey took much of the credit for the action, because he killed many of the fugitives from the battle. Pompey was granted a magnificent triumph for victories over Sertorius and Spain, while Crassus could not even ask for a triumph for a victory in a servile war, a war with slaves. He humiliatingly accepted the lesser honour, 'the ovation', comprising only a procession on foot.[7]

The Greek historian Appian, also writing in the second century CE, adds some details missing from Plutarch's account, including that the body of Spartacus was never found. Of his men:

> Splitting themselves into four groups, they continued to fight until all of them had perished – all, that is, except six thousand of them, who were taken prisoner and crucified along the whole length of the highway that ran from Capua to Rome.[8]

Although this was the last of the great slave rebellions in Roman history, the possibility of slave revolt, individual or collective, continued to haunt Roman culture, and made the task of mastery, so contradictory and strange, with its oppression and intimacies, ever more difficult.

The story of Spartacus and his army has had a long afterlife. Its modern history may go back to that avid reader of the ancients, Karl Marx. Brent Shaw records the anecdote; when Marx's daughter Jenny gave him a questionnaire in 1865, which included a question on 'his hero', he answered 'Spartacus and Kepler.'[9] And in a letter to Engels written in 1861, he wrote: 'Spartacus emerges as one of the best characters in the whole of ancient history. A great general (unlike Garibaldi), a noble character, a genuine representative of the ancient proletariat. Pompey a real shit acquired an undeserved reputation.' (Shaw, 14–15) Rosa Luxemburg and Karl Liebknecht, leftists in Germany, at the time of the First World War signed letters against the war with the name 'Spartakus,' suggesting that the proletariat of the Western powers were all slaves about to be sacrificed by the capitalist states. And they founded what they called the Spartakusbund, the Spartacist League, to resist both the war and what followed; Luxemburg and Liebknecht became martyrs to the German left, assassinated in 1919. Lenin, in *The State*, points to the example of Spartacus for contemporary proletarian revolution, seeing a class struggle in Roman antiquity between slaves and masters, and Spartacus as the Lenin of his day.

Spartacus was especially revered in the Soviet Union, serving as the object of historical studies on his uprising, and, throughout communist Eastern Europe, providing his name to sports clubs, as Stalin also took up the cause of the Roman rebellion, identifying, inaccurately but indelibly for Russian ancient history, the slave revolt as the cause of the fall of the Roman Empire, which actually took place some four hundred years later. The Soviet composer Aram Khachaturian wrote a ballet on the subject of Spartacus, which was produced continuously throughout the years of the Soviet Union. The final version, performed by the Bolshoi Ballet, was choreographed by Yuri Grigorovich. Earlier Soviet ballets had included one on the French revolution, 'Flame of Paris,' (1932). Khachaturian had traveled to Italy with a cultural delegation and was inspired by a visit to the Colosseum in Rome to return to the subject of the Roman revolutionary, relying for the most part on Plutarch's *Life of Crassus* and on Appian's version of the same events. The librettist Volkov elaborated on the narratives of the Romans, adding female characters; for Spartacus a lover, Phrygia, who is sold to Crassus, who also has a fictitious female lover, Aegina, a lustful femme fatale. Volkov also added a Judas figure, Harmodius, who betrays Spartacus because of his thwarted desire for Aegina. Christian themes echo throughout the ballet, as Spartacus casts out the capitalist traders from his camp, is betrayed by his disciples, is crucified and deposed from his cross, before an 'apotheosis' in which he undergoes metaphorical resurrection, to the music of a requiem. The ballet premiered in Leningrad in 1956, choreographed by Leonid Jacobson; it was reworked several times before it achieved a final form, first performed in 1968 and choreographed by Grigorovich, who returned it to a ballet based on character and dance, rather than massive spectacle, extras and a huge choir.

The production available on DVD was made by a Japanese company and issued in 1990, ironically thus celebrating the proletarian hero Spartacus just as the Soviet Union crumbled. The earlier productions may have differed significantly, in that the choreography seems to have staged a cruder dialectic, the agonistic confrontations between slave and Roman, Spartacus and Crassus, contrasting the sluttish Aegina, who betrays the slave army, with the virtuous and modestly dressed Phrygia, slave partner of Spartacus. The ballet climaxed with the crucifixion of Spartacus, followed by a deposition from the cross, which, in the 1990 version, has become less metaphorically Christian, setting the captured and dying Spartacus at the apex of a triangle of Roman spears. And the deposition, which still has aspects of a *pietà*, with the red robe of Spartacus trailing beneath him, ends with the hands of the slaves reaching upward toward Phrygia. The heavy-handed treatment of the dialectic, the contest between decadent Rome and proletarian slaves, ending with the metaphysical, the transcendence of Spartacus's death by a slave union of committed rebels, and coded with Christian allegory, has been somewhat muted in this performance. The ballet included not just Christian references, and fascistic marching by the Roman soldiers, but also, eventually, currents of censored Western music. The score of the duel between Spartacus and Crassus at the end of the second act, for example, incorporates allusions to the musical *West Side Story*, and the Roman orgy scenes associated with the decadent Crassus, as pointed out in the liner notes, take place to an accompaniment of Latin American rhythms, rumba and jazz trumpeting.

As well as providing a model for proletarian revolutionaries in communist societies, Spartacus had a long history of representation in novels and in film.[10] These have been explored extensively in recent scholarship, In *Spartacus: Film and History*, edited by Martin Winkler, various scholars

124

discuss both the classical version of the history of Spartacus, and its legacy.[11] There were plays and novels about the Roman slave Spartacus, including the influential *Spartaco*, published in Italian by Raffaello Giovagnoli in 1874. A long sequence of fictions and dramatic works followed, and affected the vision of Spartacus of such artists as Aram Khachaturian. Winkler lists some twelve films, eleven of which were made in Italy, and eleven of which preceded the American version.

Later novels included Arthur Koestler's *The Gladiators*, first published in Germany and translated into English in 1939. This novel by a dedicated anti-Communist explored the inevitability of dictatorship after revolution, in a thinly veiled allegory of the fate of the Soviet Union. Koestler's version of the slave rebellion, consistent with his view in *The God That Failed*, condemned Spartacus as a predecessor to Stalin and his followers as a bloodthirsty mob eventually manipulated by a power-mad Stalinist demagogue. One of the factors affecting the production of the American film *Spartacus* was a potential conflict between that film and another, based on Koestler's novel, with a script written by the screenwriter Abraham Polonsky, who had been blacklisted during the communist witch-hunts of the McCarthyist period, during the 1950s in the United States.

Especially important for the Dalton Trumbo and Kirk Douglas film of 1960 was the novel by Howard Fast, *Spartacus*, published by the author himself in 1951. Fast had been blacklisted and spent time in jail, and could not find a publisher for his work. His *Spartacus* condemns the decadent, homosexual, incestuous and corrupt Romans, setting against the backdrop of their corruption the noble slaves led by Spartacus, who left their 'plantations' to join his struggle. He incorporates the growing interest of the American left in civil rights and anti-racism in the southern states into his novel by including in his cast of characters an African gladiator, Draba, who rather than killing his comrade Spartacus in a duel to the death staged for the Romans, jumps into the midst of the spectators. Fast also includes among the gladiators a Jewish slave who had fought for freedom in Galilee, with a nod to the recent foundation of the state of Israel.

When Kirk Douglas decided to produce and star in a film about Spartacus, he deliberately used Fast's somewhat idealizing novel and employed as screen-writer Dalton Trumbo, who also had been blacklisted as one of the famed 'Hollywood Ten,' and had not been named in movie credits as a screen-writer since 1947, although he had written scripts attributed to others. The film, although it persists in presenting an idealized portrait of Spartacus himself, fell short of Fast's vision for it, and Kirk Douglas too was disap-pointed in the outcome, in part the result of a tug-of-war among screen-writers, film directors and producers, the movie studios and those who exhibited the films in theatres. As Maria Wyke shows:

> In Trumbo's view, the omission from the film of any sequence displaying a significant victory for the slave army emasculated the heroic gladiator, while the decision to close the film with his cruci-fixion – against all the historical evidence and against the narrative closure of both book and screenplay – created an 'irritating allusion' to Christ (which appeared to remodel the political militant as spir-itual martyr).[12]

Such conservative Christian groups as the Legion of Decency threatened the studios, television had arrived as a challenge to the survival of the movie industry, producers and studios invested vast sums in these historical epic films, and the industry worked under the scrutiny of right-wing govern-ment groups and the Production Code. The result, in the case of *Spartacus*, was a work of art as conceived by a committee, without the powerful crit-ical edge of Fast's novel or Trumbo's screenplay. The original director, Anthony Mann, was fired by Douglas, and replaced by Stanley Kubrick, who had his own vision of what the film should be. Mann had wanted it to focus on the physical hardships of slavery, and, in the earlier scenes of the film, the sequence in the Libyan mines, for example, he shows the punishing toll taken on the slaves' bodies as they struggle silently to satisfy the slave-drivers. Stanley Kubrick had a more pessimistic, cynical view of the narrative of Spartacus, which worked against Douglas's wish to project Spartacus's heroism, and the two struggled throughout the filming, especially concerning the issue of whether or not the slaves' victories over the Romans, expensive battle scenes, would be shot. Although the film has been a great favourite with audiences and was shown often, for example, in the former Soviet Union and Eastern Europe, it is somewhat muddled in its representation of the history of Spartacus.

Consistently with Fast's homophobia, the bisexuality of the decadent Romans is represented negatively. Recent viewers remember the scene, once cut, now restored, between Lawrence Olivier and Tony Curtis, the former playing Crassus, the latter the Sicilian slave Antoninus; Olivier, in the characteristically ambiguous manner of Fast's novel's personae, obliquely attempts to seduce his 'body' slave, dressed only in shorts, inquiring whether he prefers 'oysters or snails.' Crassus insists: 'it is all a matter of taste,' not a question of morals. 'My taste includes both snails and oysters,' recalling the vulnerability of Greek and Roman slaves to the sexual desires of their masters and mistresses. Then, again obliquely threatening, he goes to the window and gazes out at a panorama including marching Roman soldiers and expresses awe at Rome, 'the power that sits astride the world like a colossus.' He submits that there is no way to withstand her: 'You must serve her, you must abase yourself before her, you must grovel at her feet, you must love her.' He turns, and Antoninus has disappeared. Cut to a shot from above of Roman soldiers approaching an escarpment guarded by the slave rebels, and, in the next scene, Antoninus has joined the happy band of slaves in the forest, dressed like proto-hippies, celebrating and enjoying a bohemian life without cares and with a collective sharing of labour.

The film has its sentimental aspects, and to some degree preserves the attitudes of Fast's *Spartacus*, the homophobia, commitment to anti-racism, and a vision of the slaves as an ancient proletariat. But, as noted earlier, it is marked by an aura of Christianizing sentiment that falsifies the historical record. After an overture, the opening scenes show Spartacus labouring in an African mine, while a voice-over announces the setting of the narrative, 'in the last century before the birth of the new faith called Christianity, which was destined to overthrow the pagan tyranny of Rome.' The masculine voice comments that Rome was 'stricken with the disease called human slavery,' and notes that the age of the emperors, of dictatorship, was already imminent. Spartacus was born in Thrace as a slave, and 'sold to living death before his thirteenth birthday,' sent to work the mines of Libya and 'dreaming the death of slavery, two thousand years before it would die.' These observations both suggest that Christianity will change the world for the better, but also ensure that the viewer knows that it took another two millennia before slavery was eradicated in the new world. Spartacus himself is characterized as someone defined by his compassion for the sufferings of others; he fights to defend another slave in Libya, and, as he falls in love with Varinia, who has to enter the cell and be sexually used by 'the Spaniard 'Spartacus asks, 'Did he hurt you?'

Jean Simmons, as Spartacus's partner Varinia, with her saintly and demure demeanour, prepares the way for the last scene when, carrying her newborn child in her arms, she looks up at Spartacus, crucified with all his men, never betrayed by them, shows him his infant son and promises him that the son, who is free, will remember him. She seems to ride off into a Christian sunset in an anachronistic ending that casts its glow backwards over all that has preceded. Christian monotheism is thus imposed on the polytheism of the Thracian slave and his comrades, or on the atheism of the proletariat, in a mood that seems caught like a contagion from such earlier and later Biblical epics as *The Robe*, *Demetrius and the Gladiators*, and *Ben-Hur* which was, we must remember, originally written in novel form, *A Story of the Christ*. These narratives themselves often had their origins in Victorian paintings like those of Alma-Tadema, and in nineteenth-century novels.

Spartacus, if it has its allegorical meanings in relation to the civil rights struggle in America, looking forward in 1960, and back, to the red-baiting and anti-trade union witch-hunts of the 1950s, also looks further back, as mentioned earlier, not only to the foundation of the modern state of Israel, but also to the events of the holocaust carried out by Nazi Germany. Spartacus labours in the sands of Egypt like an Old Testament slave. There are echoes of other films as well; like the documentary masterpiece *Grass*,

Spartacus shows great masses of people carrying out their daily lives on a trek through unfamiliar territory, walking across fords of rivers, up mountainsides, in snow, burying a child, milking a goat. And, after the defeat of the slave army, we see the bodies of the dead piled up like holocaust victims, men, women and children, stacked together, jumbled like refuse, as in *Night and Fog*.

In the scene in which the Romans, who have finally defeated Spartacus's army, demand that they surrender their leader, there is an echo of a story, apocryphal or not, told of the Second World War. In the film *Exodus*, also released in 1960, a girl recounts that in Denmark, when the Nazis occupied, they required every Jew to wear a star of David on a yellow armband. The next day, the King of Denmark appeared with the star of David on his arm; all the Danes followed his lead, and all wore the star. In the parallel scene in Spartacus, when asked 'who is Spartacus?' a man steps from the crowd and says: 'I am Spartacus.' Another follows: 'I'm Spartacus.' And so on until each one claims to be Spartacus, and all, including Spartacus, are crucified. The message of solidarity and loyalty conveyed by this scene is one of the most powerful legacies of the film.

Part of its appeal is the love story between Spartacus and the serene and beatific Varinia. But there is also an attempt to exemplify the collective values and community spirit of a traditional left. At times, the scenes of the slave camp echo moments in the film made of John Steinbeck's *Grapes of Wrath*, which presents despair and hope in the circumstances of the great depression in the US, touching as that film does on families, old and young women labouring for their children in difficult circumstances.

Although the narrative depicts the eventual defeat of Spartacus and his army, in the film, Spartacus tells Crassus, after he is forced to kill his friend and beloved Antoninus in one last gladiatorial combat: 'he'll come back, and he'll be millions.' And there are other premonitions of the eventual victory of those who resist tyranny; the victorious slave army enters the city of Metapontum, in scenes that resemble the Americans entering liberated Paris. The emphasis here is on collectivity, the group of followers that Spartacus assembles. As they march toward Rome, we see the great train of slaves, composed of the many, an old man, babies, women and other children.

Themes of the left are introduced: incipient feminism, as one old woman defends women's presence in the camp of the resisters, and she reminds Spartacus that a woman bore him; we see women baking bread, making candles, caring for children. There is a trade-union aspect to the assembled masses; slaves arrive with skills, a carpenter, a mason, a chief steward. And the 'bread and roses' issue is touched upon. Antoninus, singer of songs – 'I also juggle' – performs magic. The army needs not just soldiers, but also poetry.

The film throughout tries to emphasize the collective nature of suffering and of resistance; Spartacus fights for the other slaves in Libya, and although he is the movie star, the movie's star, he is represented as one of many, always part of the whole, and his followers demonstrate their commitment to the common struggle, to solidarity and loyalty; this representation of the hero is different from that of Khachaturian's rigorously dialectical ballet, where the focus is on the principal dancer and the solos and duets of the major characters, where the chorus, the *corps de ballet* is made up of anonymous slaves, shepherds and shepherdesses, indistinguishable from the chorus of soldiers except by costume and style of dance. *Spartacus* is a film touched by the progressive activism of the thirties, the communist resistance to the sufferings of the great depression, the persecution of leftists after the second world war and also by the coming social movements, feminism, the civil rights struggle and the anti-authoritarianism of the 1960s that contributed to organized opposition to the war in Vietnam. The ancient slave rebellion is a vehicle for the film-makers' exploration of these issues, and, although it describes a defeat, it tries to project a legacy of continuity, through Spartacus' and Varinia's son and a genealogy of resistance to 'tyranny' that leads to the film's present and beyond it.

Gladiator

In the years after *Spartacus*, other movies set in ancient Rome appeared; among them was the controversial, pornographic *Caligula*, based on a script written by Gore Vidal and produced by Bob Guccione, publisher of *Penthouse* magazine. Filmed essentially as an occasion for X-rated scenes of Roman orgies, the film starred Malcolm McDowell as the ill-fated emperor. It featured the passionate love affair of Caligula, 'little boots,' with his sister Drusilla, much explicit sex of many varieties and a great deal of violence, including a building façade-sized mowing machine that severed heads of enemies buried in the sand in the arena. Little attention was paid to the fate of slaves; they were shown as voyeurs in intimate scenes between the emperor and his sister, or casually leaning against walls in decorative near-nakedness. The fantasy of beginnings, of liberation from enslavement so typical of historical epics, has no place here. Bondage and cruelty, the trappings of sado-masochism, dominate rather than the heroic escapades of men fleeing enslavement. The only hint of such motives occurs in a scene in which the philosophic Nerva, played by John Gielgud, advisor to the decadent emperor Tiberius, cuts his wrists and, as his blood ebbs away in the conveniently transparent bath, is pushed under the surface by the soon-to-be emperor Caligula. (According to our historical sources, he committed suicide by starving himself to death, obviously a less visually gratifying spectacle.) The musical score, strangely, uses the music of Aram Khachaturian and continuously echoes a mix of *My Way*, famously sung by Frank Sinatra, with *Stormy Weather*, another classic of the African-American repertoire. The film caused a scandal when it was released in 1979. It is significant here only because its steamy atmosphere, and in particular the incestuous link between emperor and sister, have their shadowy effect on the film *Gladiator*, in which the emperor Commodus lusts vainly after his sister, and where the perversity and kinkiness always resorted to in American depictions of Rome follow on the much more explicit sexuality, homoerotic as well as heterosexual, of the earlier film.

Gladiator, released in 2000, the year of the millennium, builds on the legacy of other movies representing ancient history, including *Ben-Hur*, and Anthony Mann's *The Fall of the Roman Empire*, as well as Stanley Kubrick's *Spartacus*. A Hollywood movie directed by the Australian Ridley Scott, this film stresses not the collective sufferings and courage of a slave army, but the heroism of a noble individual. Both Scott and Walter Parkes, one of the producers of *Gladiator*, point to the effect on them of Jean-Leon Gerome's painting of 1872, '*Pollice Verso*', 'Thumbs Down', which depicts the end of a gladiatorial duel in which a victorious fighter looks up to the emperor for his verdict, life or death.[13] Scott is credited with reviving the 'toga-and-sandal' film, the epic film set in ancient Rome, which had fallen out of favour after the great success of *Spartacus* in 1960.

Scott also discusses his motives in accepting the assignment of directing *Gladiator*:

Mass entertainment provides a visceral experience of things you can't have, or can't do. 'Escapism' is a word with bad connotations. I prefer 'transported', 'elevated', or 'taken on a journey!' (9)

The director of *Blade Runner* (1982), based on the dystopic story of Philip K. Dick, *Do Androids Dream of Electric Sheep*, nonetheless provides more than escapism in this ultimately tragic narrative of a dispossessed heir to the Roman empire who becomes a slave, a gladiator, and brings down an emperor only to die himself in the arena. The screenwriter David Franzoni described his intentions:

The movie is about our culture, our society: promoter Proximo (Oliver Reed) is sort of a Mike Ovitz, and Commodus (Joaquin Phoenix) is sort of a Ted Turner. And Maximus (Russell Crowe) is the hero we all wish ourselves to be: the guy who can rise above the mess that is modern society.[14]

Even though we might not all want to be that 'guy', *Gladiator* was an enormous success throughout the world.

In this film, in contrast to *Spartacus*, the focus is on the heroic, alienated individual. Maximus, its central character, in line for power over the whole of the Roman empire, which is taken for granted as the only possible state in the world of the film, belongs to the provincial estate-owning class, and has been enlisted to fight for his emperor, Marcus Aurelius, as other generals fought in the time of the Roman Republic, most memorably Cincinnatus, a hero remembered by the founders of the American republic, to whom George Washington was compared. Such modest, austere gentleman-farmer-soldiers are by now a distant memory, nostalgically recalled not only by the several senators who appear in the film, but also by the emperor himself. Strangely enough, the senate resembles the Senate of the American Republic rather than that of ancient Rome, which was for the most part a hereditary, aristocratic body. The senator 'Gracchus,' played in the film by Derek Jacobi, says that the senate is 'chosen by the people,' a gross error, wildly ahistorical and anachronistic. Although one hardly cares if the film is historically accurate in its details, this issue does affect the politics of the twenty-first century representation of Rome, and makes its allusions to American politics more pointed. The premise is that after receiving imperial power from Marcus Aurelius, the general Maximus, adored by his soldiers, will return his nation to its republic and restore sovereignty to its senators. This fantasy affects the 'Republican,' in the Ronald Reagan sense, mood of the film, its elegiac and nostalgic yearning for a John Wayne-like hero, a Ronald Reagan even, who will restore the 'republic,' the domination of the senior, wealthier, often more conservative body of the (American) legislature, those military heroes 'chosen by the people.' Rather than a populist fantasy, this is conservative militarist nostalgia.

Displaced by Commodus, who murders his father Marcus Aurelius, and thwarts the plan to restore the senate to republican power, Maximus barely evades execution by Commodus's men. He falls into slavery but, in a sort of family romance plot, he remains stoic and noble, a general and emperor in disguise, like Judah Ben-Hur, who lives some time as a slave in the movie named for him, until a Roman aristocrat recognizes his true but concealed nobility, and adopts him. Maximus, in *Gladiator*, spends some time as slave, but he never shares the mentality or the ambitions of his fellow slaves. He is their general, and, in the conspiracy that emerges, including his slave Cicero, along with the emperor's sister and the senator Gracchus, his fellow slave gladiators become his infantry as he reminds them of the motto of his army: 'Strength and honour.' Their status as gladiators overrides their status as slaves, and they become his soldiers. There is never any sense that slavery itself is a wrong; rather, it is the enslavement of the free, noble, heroic individual that is to be overturned. Maximus is never really one of the slaves, but always a more talented, successful, supremely violent gladiator fueled by his rage. His aspiration is to revenge the murder of his wife and son by Commodus, and this dream drives him forward, but his only hope of reunion with them lies in the afterlife. And the goal of returning to republican rule, dear to Marcus Aurelius and to senators who are minor characters in the film, seems to mean little to him, although the ambiguous ending leaves the audience thinking that such a historical impossibility might have taken place.

The film focuses on Maximus's role as a gladiator, rather than as a slave. He suffers routine slavish humiliations, and forms some kind of bond with a Numidian fellow-slave, Juba, who buries the figurines of Maximus's wife and child in the arena in which he died, and promises to meet him in the afterlife, but 'not yet,' as he seems to smile at the prospect of returning to his family in Africa, freed in the turmoil of the republican plot to depose Commodus. But the splendor, blood and terror of the arena preoccupy the film-makers of this epic, which becomes an exploration of athleticism, special effects and spectacle, rather than a myth about worker solidarity. At one point, after an especially bloody and successful slaughter of other gladiators by Maximus, in a provincial arena, he expresses his contempt for the mob, the crowd, blood-thirstily cheering him: 'Are you not entertained?' And then he spits at the audience in the ring. The film consistently portrays the crowds of spectators as rabble, the proletariat thirsty for blood. Proximo, the slaveowner and gladiator-master, a freed slave and former gladiator himself, at first resists Maximus's request for assistance in the conspiracy against Commodus, saying 'I'm an entertainer,' although eventually he is drawn into the republican plot when Maximus reveals that Commodus murdered his own father, Marcus Aurelius, the emperor who had freed Proximo, and allowed him to own others who could entertain the mob. Peter W. Rose, in his work on the politics of the film, points to this aspect of the film-makers' ideology:

> To Scott, the fundamental flaw in the system is the mob, the people of Rome seen as the audience in the arena, who in turn stand in for the cinema audience. This self-reflexive aspect, absent from *The Fall of the Roman Empire*, is central to *Gladiator*.[15]

The contempt of the film-makers, implicit in their condemnation of the rabble, did not prevent the huge, international commercial success of *Gladiator*. If we seek some element of potential audience appreciation beyond escapism, ignorance or masochism, we might see it in the simplicity of the solutions offered and the persistent fantasy of the lone individual who can bring down an empire.

Carlin Barton, in her wonderful book *Sorrows of the Ancient Romans*, speaks to the strange and extreme life of the early years of the Roman empire, especially the first century BCE and the first two centuries of the common era.[16]

> [Hers] is a book about the emotional life of the ancient Romans. In particular, it is about the extremes of despair, desire, fascination, and envy, and the ways in which these emotions organized the world and directed the actions of the ancient Romans.
>
> This is a book about the gladiator and the monster, the most conspicuous of the figures through which these extremes of emotions were enacted and expressed.(3)

For the ancient Romans, gladiators were bearers of humiliation and exaltation. Marcus Aurelius, the Stoic emperor who left behind his meditations, commented on the futility of clinging to life and saw such futility in the gladiator: 'To continue to be such as you have hitherto been and to be torn in pieces and defiled in such a life, is the character of a very stupid man and one overfond of his life, and like those half-devoured fighters with wild beasts, who, though covered with wounds and gore, still entreat to be kept to the following day, though they will be exposed in the same state to the same claws and bites.' (10.8) Such men are fools, mistaking the pain of life and desiring only to hold on to what they know; the emperor's comments express the contempt, identification and pity felt by the serene philosopher for such mortal warriors and slaves.

There were aristocratic gladiators, those who chose to abase themselves in the arena, to provide entertainment and a spectacle of despair and desire before the Roman crowd. It is this, it seems, which fascinated Ridley Scott, who took the plot of Anthony Mann's *Fall of the Roman Empire* and turned it into a spectacle about the noble gladiator. For his film, the fact of Maximus's slavery is almost incidental. Masses, slave or free, barely figure in its iconography. Maximus, the tragic hero, stands for an imperial power, for a rugged heroism untouched by sentiments of solidarity with any others but his immediate family. It is a film appropriate to the post-Reagan years, to the Bush years, to a period in which the United States felt comfortable with its empire, and nostalgic for the simplicities of heroes like John Wayne.[17] Arthur Pomeroy concludes: 'we are probably justified to regard *Gladiator* as commending not an outright Fascist ideology but a neo-conservative rural utopianism . . .'[18]

The monumentality of the great capital city, Rome, in this film echoes images familiar from the Nazi Third Reich and the fascism of Mussolini's city. As the gladiators enter the city, fresh from their provincial testing in North Africa, which has a peculiarly anachronistic Muslim quality, they are awed by the majesty of the city. The special effects create a gray city, with long lines of monumental buildings and soldiers stretching off into the distance; the formal aspects invoke Leni Riefenstahl's *Triumph of the Will*, echoing her images in black and white. The eagles of the Roman standards, the uniforms of the legions, the spaces of the monumental city, refer not to the massive structures of the earlier twentieth-century epics, set in the ancient near east, but to the twenties, thirties and forties of the twentieth century and the dark legacy of the second world war. This Rome is akin to Hitler's Berlin and Mussolini's Rome, a site of dictatorship in which Commodus stands in for the tyrants of Europe, and Maximus is a heroic general of the Resistance or the *partigiani*.

The account of the computer-generation of the imagery of this film provides intriguing reading:

[T]he VFX [visual and special effects] team needed a 'robust strategy' for multiplying their 2,000 extras into some 70,000 screaming, gesticulating fans. (121)

The film-makers made 'tiles' of the smaller crowd, and placed them in a three-dimensional model of the Colosseum. 'To make those tiles, the ... team shot crowd performers against a greenscreen with bluescreen slashes of colour in their costumes.' This allowed the special effects workers to recolour the members of the crowd, 'for variety,' as they captured 'each extra in a range of poses: staring, cheering, nonchalantly talking, thumbs up, thumbs down.' (121) The vague, blurry sense of the crowd, then, experienced by the viewer, comes from this manipulation of a few thousand extras, who stand in for the masses, who are given bread along with their circus, and are always potential enemies of the hero, in fact, to be swayed by the spectacle of death before them, unlike the real masses of *Spartacus*, which represents not just the opposing Roman legions, but also the individual faces and figures of the slave army and its accompanying slave community.

In one of the scenes of gladiatorial combat in *Gladiator*, set in the computer-restored, immense edifice of the Colosseum, Maximus leads his troops, his gladiators, by giving commands as to his soldiers. In a staged combat, meant to represent the defeat of the Carthaginians by the Roman legions of Scipio, the hero leads his 'Carthaginian' troops to victory and humiliates the master of the games, who had promised a Roman triumph for the emperor Commodus. In the last scene of the film, we are left with the individual, the stark isolation of this hero, who kills the emperor and dies alone in the arena. Though he is 'a slave more powerful than the emperor,' it is as general and nobleman that he triumphs, not as slave. And his own slave Cicero, who remains devoted and loyal, continues to serve him until his death. This is tragic, vigilante heroism of the Mad Max variety, and the film sometimes tilts into the realm of science fiction, or of a Felliniesque surrealism. The film-makers delighted not only in grotesque bodies, but also in the superior technology of well-armed soldiers who defeat the Germans, for example, in the early scenes of the movie, reminiscent of the dark forests of Mann's beginning to *The Fall of the Roman Empire*, where the armies fight through falling snow. The resourceful, violent loner survives through using his wits and his body, until, at last, he is brought down, sacrificing himself nobly but without hope of an aftermath. Martin Winkler points to the many American films starring such a protagonist, from *Braveheart* to *Erin Brockovich*; 'These and other comparable heroes all come from the same romantic American mould, according to which rebels, loners or outcasts, follow a vision, dream, or calling to build or achieve something great.'[19]

The emperor Commodus was actually strangled to death by his masseur, a man, a slave named Narcissus. According to the third-century historian Herodian, who gives the fullest and most sensational of accounts, Commodus's plot, with orders to execute his mistress Marcia and other subordinates, was betrayed by a boy, a naked slave dressed in jewels, like others the Roman elite used as living toys:

> After writing on the tablet he [Commodus] left it on the couch, thinking no one would come into his room. But he forgot about the little boy, who was one of those that fashionable Roman fops are pleased to keep in their households running around without any clothes on, decked out in gold and fine jewels. Commodus had such a favourite, whom he often used to sleep with. He used to call him Philocommodus ('love of Commodus'), a name to show his fondness for the boy. (1.17)[20]

This child slave picked up Commodus's orders, Marcia took them from the child, and fearing for her own life, she poisoned the emperor and then had

Commodus strangled by his masseur. (Herodian 1.16–17) The cinematic scene of the duel between Maximus and Commodus did not occur, although Commodus did enjoy 'fighting' in the arena, providing a weird spectacle of the emperor debased and exalted. As Barton puts it:

> The gladiators were seen as salacious libertines. Simultaneously . . . they were the models of a severe asceticism: there were no more austerely disciplined soldiers in the Roman world than the greatest gladiators trained in the imperial *ludi*. No other figure in Roman society embodied, in quite such extremes, punishment and impunity, constraint and abandon, asceticism and profligacy. (48)

Athletes, film stars, the subjects of almost-pornographic biographies on television, there are such figures in public life in the present, in the Western world. But few have the stoic, manly, pious, devoted humility and violence of the heroes of Westerns, or of earlier toga epics. Maximus stands alone, redeeming the figure of the slave and the gladiator with a monomaniacal and private obsession with vengeance. The fantasy is that such a man can bring down a corrupt political system and restore family values, an uncontaminated empire and republicans, a fantasy with extraordinary potency in a post-feminist, imperial and globalizing world. There is no address to the question of the many slaves who inhabit the world in this film. Their existence is accepted as a matter of fact; Maximus's slave Cicero accepts his fate as a proper Stoic should. It is only the improper enslavement of the great man, the great general, the free farmer of his estates, that triggers the plot of this film, and, when he dies, although there is a false promise of a return to senatorial rule, this means nothing for the slaves of Rome. And this film, made at the turn of the millennium, offers nothing to those enslaved in the present, nor to those who would imagine a better world than the one we inhabit, still dominated by empire and impregnable to the lone, alienated heroes of cinematic fantasy. The hope of change resides rather in remembering many acts of resistance and resilience, by the millions of slaves who have lived and died in slavery and by some who escaped to freedom.

EPILOGUE

There is a secret agreement between past generations and the present one. Our coming was expected on earth. Like every generation that preceded us, we have been endowed with a *weak* Messianic power, a power to which the past has a claim. That claim cannot be settled cheaply.

— *Walter Benjamin*

Antiquity lives on, and demands our attention. It is implicated in our cultural productions, in structures of thought and perception. It is also an inexhaustible intellectual reservoir. What I have wanted to stress throughout this book is that antiquity is not only the site of ancient slavery, but that it also offers us alternative political imaginings. If we encounter the sufferings of ancient slaves as we study the ancient world of Greece and Rome and a legacy of justifications for enslaving human beings, turning them into commodities, into objects, into possessions, we also find the beginnings of resistance to the idea that one person can own another. It is the regrettable persistence of slavery but also the ambivalent and enduring complexity of antiquity that I have sought to convey.

I began with slavery in the present, in our current circumstances of globalization, in which there are vast currents of exchange, interdependency and a struggle for domination, as well as pockets of ancient traditions, some benignly resisting transformation, others concealing circumstances of terrible exploitation and hopelessness. It is easy to comfort ourselves that the scourge of slavery has been long eradicated from the world, that the abolitionist movements of the enlightenment long ago freed all the slaves. Yet, as I have tried to show, relying on the research of others, there are still slaves, millions of slaves, slaves in every nation on earth. And our failure to recognize this fact makes it less likely that they will be freed from bondage, whether theirs is domestic slavery, agricultural labour, sexual enslavement or one of the many other forms, legally explicit or not, which keep people in bondage.

Another issue which has concerned me here is the relationship between so-called 'race', that is, ethnic or other forms of difference, and the likelihood of enslavement. People of colour, people traditionally lowest in the social hierarchies of national or religious or other formations, have always been more vulnerable to enslavement, by their own kind or by strangers. I have sought to examine some of the ideologies that justify such domination of the many by the few, and to look at the ways in which women, racial 'others', people from the southern nations, the poor, fall into the categories of the enslaveable, in the present and in the great slave projects of the early modern and modern periods.

One of the lasting elements of the legacy of Greek antiquity is the formulation of the concept of natural slavery by the philosopher Aristotle. Like many of the other Greeks of the classical period, though not all, he conveniently saw the barbarians, the foreigners surrounding Greece, the foreigners living among the Greeks, as inferior, needing the guidance and direction of the naturally superior Greek master, benefiting from the relationship of master to slave. The Romans inherited this view, which justified their ownership and exploitation of the Greeks themselves, among others, who fell into the state of enslavement. And, in the great surge of exploration and conquest that began the early modern period of European colonialism, this idea provided the justification for vast new projects of enslavement, in which the customary slavery of black Africans was transformed into a machine for generating capital for the colonizing powers of Europe. The barbarians of the ancient Greeks became the Africans of the

Americas, transported to serve new masters and to colonize and develop the new world. The slave masters of the Americans inherited not only the notion of natural slavery, that some human beings naturally deserved enslavement and benefited from it, but also that slavery itself was natural, as inevitable as the political systems of empire, republicanism, democracy and monarchy that came down to them from classical antiquity.

Along with the naturalization of slavery came other vestigial notions deeply imbedded in the Western tradition, ideas about the necessity for hierarchy in the state, the control and domination of the slavish lower classes by elite rulers. Concepts of self-mastery, the need to enslave one's passions, to master the psyche, to govern one's body as a master governs a slave, to obey one's superiors, especially the divinities and, in the case of the monotheisms of the Abrahamic tradition, Christianity, Judaism and Islam, to obey the one god as a slave obeys her master. Rather than providing modes of resistance or escape from slavery, religion often reinforced the chasm between masters and slaves.

As I said above, the legacy from classical antiquity remains ambivalent and complex. Along with the rationalizations for natural slavery and for the naturalness of slavery, comes an inheritance of resistance to enslavement, found in the myth of the Hebrew slaves who escaped from bondage, in the will of the ancient Athenians to escape enslavement to the Persian emperor, in the ancient philosophers' cultivation of habits of mind that left them indifferent to the bodily sufferings of torture and enslavement, and in the many examples of slave flight and rebellion, including those of Aristonikos in Asia Minor, and Spartacus in southern Italy. If most of the lasting evidence concerning the ancient worlds of the Israelites, the Greeks and the Romans comes down to us explicitly taking the position of the slave owners, the masters, we still find evidence of hopes for freedom and an unwillingness to surrender to domination, to undergo social death, to experience slavery's erasure of history and genealogy, to submit to a life of dishonour. The very notion of freedom, it is often claimed, came into being in the circumstances of the Athenians' struggle against enslavement to the Persian emperor, and this must be set alongside democracy as one of the enduring elements of the legacy from antiquity, to counter Aristotle's concept of natural slavery.

These ideas, contradictory and transmuted by the events of the long history that intervenes between the ancient world of the Greeks and Romans and our present, persist in our cultural practices and productions in the present. Racism survives, bolstered however unconsciously by ideas inherited from the barbaric past. And we see in the industries of thana-tourism and in the cinema, to take the examples discussed in the last chapter, the rewritings and transformations of events from the past that haunt the present and the future. Tourists visit the slave markets of the modern period, imagining themselves differently, no doubt, depending on their situation in the present, no doubt also unconsciously caught up in fantasies of domination and submission. In such films as *Spartacus* and *Gladiator*, so different in their representations of slavery, the earlier film presenting the slave army as a multiracial collective led by a Christ-like hero, the latter a fantasy of Mad Max-like individual heroism and exis-tential self-sacrifice, mass audiences continue to visit not only the tragic past of slavery in antiquity, but also the dreams of freedom of slaves long dead, themes that speak to current circumstances of political despair and hope, of escape and commitment.

Our readings of history, especially of the Greek and Roman past, can never exhaust the richness of its legacies, for good and ill. Antiquity changes as the present changes, can never be caught in its entirety, made to surrender up its truths; it is not a dead past, but an ever-changing past that teaches us about the present and the future as much as about the remote past. We live ephemerally, poised in an ever-vanishing present, shaped by the past and ignorant of the future. The voices of many slaves, living and dead, survive as part of the noise and music of our existence. The past is indelibly marked by slavery, its myths of conquest, empire and domination, its stories of resistance, survival and hopes for freedom. Slavery is implicated in what we know of globalization, ideologies of race, of identity and self-hood, religious fundamentalisms, colonialism and the construction of the world as we know it. If what we owe to the slaves of the past is listening, recognition, a remembering of their suffering and courage, we can also commit ourselves to ending slavery in all its variations, in the present and in the future.

SOME SUGGESTIONS FOR FURTHER READING

Kevin Bales and Becky Cornell, *Slavery Today* (Toronto and Berkeley: 2008)

Ira Berlin, *Many Thousands Gone: The First Two Centuries of Slavery in North America* (Cambridge, Mass.: 1998)

Robin Blackburn, *The Making of New World Slavery: From the Baroque to the Modern, 1492–1800* (London: 1997), and *The Overthrow of Colonial Slavery, 1776–1848* (London: 1989)

Douglas Blackmon, *Slavery by Another Name: The Re-Enslavement of Black Americans from the Civil War to World War II* (New York: 2008)

Keith Bradley, *Slaves and Masters in the Roman Empire* (New York and Oxford, 1987)

Page duBois, *Slaves and Other Objects* (Chicago: 2003)

Peter Garnsey, *Ideas of Slavery from Aristotle to Augustine* (Cambridge: 1996)

Saidiya Hartman, *Scenes of Subjection: Terror, Slavery, and Self-Making in Nineteenth-Century America* (New York: 1997)

Sandra Joshel and Sheila Murnaghan, eds., *Women and Slaves in Greco-Roman Culture* (London: 1998)

Marcus Rediker, *The Slave Ship: A Human History* (New York: 2007)

Maria Wyke, *Projecting the Past: Ancient Rome, Cinema, and History* (New York: 1997)

NOTES

Chapter I

1   Kevin Bales and Zoe Trodd, eds., *To Plead Our Own Cause: Personal Stories by Today's Slaves* (Ithaca, New York: Cornell University Press, 2008), 99–101

2   *Lysias,* with an English translation by W.R.M. Lamb (Cambridge, Mass.: Harvard University Press, 1930)

3   William Morris, ed., *The American Heritage Dictionary of the English Language* (New York: Houghton Mifflin, 1973)

4   Kevin Bales and Becky Cornell, *Slavery Today* (Toronto and Berkeley: Groundwood Books and House of Anansi Press, 2008), 9. Page numbers in the text refer to previously cited volumes.

5   Orlando Patterson, *Slavery and Social Death: A Comparative Study* (Cambridge, Mass.: Harvard University Press, 1982)

6   *The Narrative of the Life of Frederick Douglass, An American Slave, Written by Himself,* ed. Benjamin Quarles (Cambridge, Mass.: Harvard University Press, 1988), 148. The surname Douglass was suggested by Johnson, who had been reading the 'Lady of the Lake.'

7   Patterson. On this point see also Kurt Raaflaub, *The Discovery of Freedom in Ancient Greece,* rev. ed., trans. by Renate Franciscono (Chicago: University of Chicago Press, 2004 [1985])

8   Orlando Patterson, *Freedom* vol. 1: *Freedom in the Making of Western Culture* (New York: BasicBooks, 1991), xiii.

9   On these questions, see Veena Das, Arthur Kleinman, Mamphela Ramphele, and Pamela Reynolds, eds., *Violence and Subjectivity* (Berkeley: University of California Press, 2000)

10   On ancient slavery, see Jean Andreau and Raymond Descat, *Esclave en Grèce et à Rome* (Paris: Hachette, 2006)

11   E. Benjamin Skinner, 'Slavery's staying power,' Opinion, *Los Angeles Times,* 23 March 2008, M1.

12   *Le Devoir de Violence* (Paris, 1968); Ouologuem, *Bound to Violence,* trans. Ralph Manheim (London, 1968) The novel is discussed by Kwame Anthony Appiah in 'Is the Post- in Postmodernism the Post- in Postcolonial?,' *Critical Inquiry* 17 (Winter 1991), 336–57.

13 'Court Rules . . ', by Lydia Polgreen, *The New York Times* 10/28/08, A6
14 *The New York Times*, New York Report, Paul Vitello, 'From the Stand, Tales of 'Modern-Day Slavery' in a Long Island Case,' Monday, 3 December 2007, A26.
15 Kevin Bales and Becky Cornell, *Slavery Today*, 108
16 David Batstone, *Not for Sale: The Return of the Global Slave Trade – and How We Can Fight It* (New York: HarperCollins, 2007), 273
17 On the sequences from slavery to Jim Crow laws to the ghetto to the criminal justice system in the United States, see Loic Wacquant,'
18 Jacques Rancière, *Disagreement: Politics and Philosophy*, trans. J. Rose (Minneapolis: University of Minnesota Press, 1999 [1995]), 126
19 Giorgio Agamben, *Homo Sacer: Sovereign Power and Bare Life*, trans. D. Heller-Roazen (Stanford: Stanford University Press, 1998 [1995]), 133–4
20 Alain Badiou, *Saint Paul: The Foundation of Universalism*, trans. R. Brassier (Stanford: Stanford University Press, 2003 [1997]), 6.
21 David Batstone, *Not for Sale*, 255–6. The story of Given also appears in Cornell and Bales, 77–8
22 Kevin Bales, *Disposable People: New Slavery in the Global Economy* (Berkeley: University of California Press, 1999), 8–9.
23 Kwame Anthony Appiah, 'A Slow Emancipation,' *The New York Times Magazine*, March 18 2007, 15–17; passage cited, 16.
24 Ira Berlin, *Many Thousands Gone: The First Two Centuries of Slavery in North America* (Cambridge, Mass.: Belknap Press of Harvard University Press, 1998), 9–10
25 Stanley Wolpert, *A New History of India*, sixth edition (Oxford: Oxford University Press, 2000), 32.
26 James C. Scott, *Domination and the Arts of Resistance: Hidden Transcripts* (New Haven: Yale University Press, 1990), 117. Scott's work is an invaluable compendium of the ways in which dominated persons, and those who dominate them, produce 'hidden transcripts,' forms of self-presentations not exposed in the 'official' settings of everyday life.

Chapter 2

1 There is a vast bibliography on this question. I can only note those works that I found most useful, and that themselves contain bibliographies to lead the reader to further study.
2 See Arnaldo Momigliano, *The Development of Greek Biography* (Cambridge, Mass.: Harvard University Press, 1971)
3 On William Hill Brown's *The Power of Sympathy*, arguably the first American novel, published in the 1790s, see Julia Stern, *The Plight of Feeling: Sympathy and Dissent in the Early American Novel* (Chicago: The University of Chicago Press, 1997), 22–26: 'white male citizens ostensibly opposed to the practice of slavery in fact depend on it for their own (paradoxical) self-definition as members of a morally democratic elite.' (26)
4 Sherley Anne Williams, *Dessa Rose* (New York: William Morrow, 1986), 23
5 Arna Bontemps, ed., *Great Slave Narratives* (Boston: Beacon Press, 1969), 5.

6   See Marcus Rediker, *The Slave Ship: A Human History* (New York: Viking, 2007), and Stephanie Smallwood, *Saltwater Slavery: A Middle Passage from Africa to American Diaspora* (Cambridge, Mass.: Harvard University Press, 2008)

7   On slave narratives, see Frances Foster,

8   D.B. Davis, *The Problem of Slavery in Western Culture* (Ithaca, N.Y.: Cornell University Press, 1966); see also *The Problem of Slavery in the Age of Revolution, 1770–1823* (Ithaca, N.Y.: Cornell University Press, 1975), *Slavery and Human Progress* (New York: Oxford University Press, 1984), and *Inhuman Bondage: The Rise and Fall of Slavery in the New World* (New York: Oxford University Press, 2006)

9   Marcus Rediker, *The Slave Ship* (New York: Viking, 2007), 5.

10   See Douglas A. Blackmon, *Slavery By Another Name: The Re-Enslavement of Black Americans from the Civil War to World War II* (New York: Doubleday, 2008)

11   Robin Blackburn, *The Making of New World Slavery: From the Baroque to the Modern, 1492–1800* (London: Verso, 1997), and *The Overthrow of Colonial Slavery, 1776–1848* (London: Verso, 1989), 39. Page numbers in the text refer to *The Making*.

12   Saidiya V. Hartman, *Scenes of Subjection: Terror, Slavery and Self-Fashioning in Nineteenth-Century America* (New York and London: Oxford University Press, 1997), 25. Bob Jones University, a fundamentalist Christian school in Greenville South Carolina, founded in 1927, banned 'interracial dating' until 2000.

13   Luis Vaz de Camoes, *The Lusiads*, trans. Landeg White (Oxford: Oxford University Press, 1997)

14   Cited in Carl J. Richard, *The Founders and the Classics, Greece, Rome, and the American Enlightenment* (Cambridge, Mass.: Harvard University Press, 1994), 96

15   Ira Berlin, *Many Thousands Gone*, 7

16   Achille Mbembe, 'Necropolitics', trans. Libby Meintjes, Public Culture 15 (2003), 11–40; passage cited, p. 21. Mbembe refers to Giorgio Agamben's *Homo Sacer*

17   See David Theo Goldberg, *The Racial State* (Malden, Mass.: Blackwell, 2002), and Susan Buck-Morss, 'Hegel and Haiti', *Critical Inquiry* 26 (2000), 821–66.

18   Harriet A. Jacobs, *Incidents in the Life of Slave Girl, Written by Herself*, ed. L. Maria Child, ed. Jean Fagan Yellin (Cambridge, Mass.: Harvard University Press, 1987)

19   James C. Scott, *Domination and the Arts of Resistance: Hidden Transcripts* (New Haven: Yale University Press, 1990)

20   *Narrative of the Life of Frederick Douglass, An American Slave, Written by Himself*, ed. Benjamin Quarles (Cambridge, Mass.: Belknap, Harvard University Press, 1988), 14.

21   Paul Gilroy, *The Black Atlantic: Modernity and Double Consciousness* (Cambridge, Mass.: Harvard University Press, 1993), 55.

22   Edward Ball, *Slaves in the Family* (New York: Ballantine Books, 1999)

23 Douglas Blackmon, *Slavery by Another Name*
24 Loic Wacquant, 'From Slavery to Mass Incarceration: Rethinking the 'race question' in the US, *New Left Review* n.s. 13 (2002), 41–60; passage quoted 41.

Chapter 3

1 'Seeing the nakedness' may refer to sexual intercourse, or simply to dishonouring the father.
2 *The New Oxford Annotated Bible, New Revised Standard Version with the Apocrypha*, 3rd edition, ed. Michael D. Coogan (Oxford: Oxford University Press, 2007, 5. All citations of the Hebrew Bible and The New Testament come from this edition.
3 Muhammad A. Dandamaev, *Slavery in Babylonia from Nabopolassar to Alexander the Great*, 2nd ed. (DeKalb, Illinois: Northern Illinois University Press, 1984), 648
4 Ibid., 488
5 Herodotus, *The Histories*, trans. Robin Waterfield, introduction and notes by Carolyn Dewald (Oxford: Oxford University Press, 1998)
6 See P. du Bois, *Centaurs and Amazons: The Prehistory of the Chain of Being* (Ann Arbor: University of Michigan Press, 1982); Edith Hall, *Inventing the Barbarian; Self-Destruction in Greek Tragedy* (Oxford: Clarendon Press, 1989)
7 The best discussion of all these issues is Peter Garnsey's *Ideas of Slavery from Aristotle to Augustine* (Cambridge: Cambridge University Press, 1996)
8 On the analogy with slavery, see Gregory Vlastos, 'Slavery in Plato's Thought,' in *Platonic Studies* (Princeton: Princeton University Press, 1973), 146–63
9 Plato, *Republic*, trans. G.M.A. Grube, rev. C.D.C. Reeve (Indianapolis, Indiana: Hackett, 1992), 261. Citations to the text of Aristotle's *Politics*, trans. H. Rackham (London: William Heinemann, 1972)
10 Benjamin Isaac, *The Invention of Racism in Classical Antiquity* (Princeton: Princeton University Press, 2004), 503
11 Euripides, *The Complete Greek Tragedies*, vol. 4, ed. D. Grene and R. Lattimore (Chicago: University of Chicago Press, 1992); *Iphigeneia in Aulis* trans. Charles R. Walker.
12 On Roman slavery in literary texts see William Fitzgerald, *Slavery and the Roman Literary Imagination* (New York: Cambridge University Press, 2000), and Kathleen McCarthy, *Slaves, Masters, and the Art of Authority in Plautine Comedy* (Princeton: Princeton University Press, 2000)
13 Moses I. Finley, *Ancient Slavery and Modern Ideology* (London: Chatto and Windus, 1980), 120
14 Cicero, 'Paradoxa Stoicorum,' *Works*, vol. 4, trans. H. Rackham (London: W. Heinemann [Loeb Classical Library], 1942)
15 Seneca, *Moral Essays*, trans. J.W. Basore (London: W. Heinemann [Loeb Classical Library], 1928)
16 David Brion Davis, *The Problem of Slavery in Western Culture* (Ithaca, New York: Cornell University Press, 1966), 83

17   Finley, *Ancient Slavery and Modern Ideology*,119.
18   See J. Albert Harrill, *Slaves in the New Testament: Literary, Social, and Moral Dimensions* (Minneapolis, Minn.: Fortress Press, 2006)
19   On this issue, see Giorgio Agamben, *The Time that Remains*
20   On Paul's universalism, see Alain Badiou, *Saint Paul*
21   See Dale Martin, *Slavery as Salvation: The Metaphor of Slavery in Pauline Christianity* (New Haven: Yale University Press, 1990)
22   John C. Calhoun, 'Speech on the Reception of Abolition Petitions,' in *Slavery Defended: The Views of the Old South*, ed. E.L. McKitrick (Englewood Cliffs, New Jersey: Prentice-Hall, 1963),13. See also Drew Gilpin Faust, ed., *The Ideology of Slavery: Proslavery Thought in the Antebellum South, 1830–1860* (Baton Rouge: Louisiana State University Press, 1981)
23   James Henry Hammond, 'Speech on the Admission of Kansas,' US Senate, March 4, 1858, from *Selections from the Letters and Speeches of the Hon. James H. Hammond, of South Caroli*na (New York, 1866), cited in McKitrick, 123.
24   Ibid., 32.
25   George Fitzhugh, *Sociology for the South, or the Failure of Free Society* (Richmond, 1854), 235
26   Caroline Winterer, *The Culture of Classicism: Ancient Greece and Rome in American Intellectual Life 1780–1910* (Baltimore: Johns Hopkins University Press, 2002), 74 and following. See also Carl Richard, *The Founders and the Classics: Greece, Rome, and the American Enlightenment* (Cambridge, Mass.: Harvard University Press, 1994): 'Some founders perceived Greek and Roman slavery as an antimodel. As early as 1765 George Mason wrote regarding the Roman republic: "One of the first signs of the decay and perhaps the primary cause of the destruction of the most flourishing government that ever existed was the introduction of great numbers of slaves, an evil very pathetically described by Roman historians."' (96)

Chapter 4

1   On the historiography of Greek and Roman slavery, see Niall McKeown, *The Invention of Ancient Slavery?* (London: Duckworth, 2007)
2   *The Odyssey of Homer*, trans. Richmond Lattimore (New York: Harper/Collins, 1975)
3   Aristotle, *The Athenian Constitution*, trans. P.J. Rhodes (Harmondsworth: Penguin, 1984), 43.
4   *Greek Lyrics*, trans. Richmond Lattimore, 2nd rev. ed. (Chicago: University of Chicago Press, 1960), 22
5   Stephen Hodkinson, *Property and Wealth in Classical Sparta* (London: 2000)
6   Paul Cartledge, *The Spartans: The World of the Warrior-Heroes of Ancient Greece* (New York: Vintage, 2004), 29
7   Carl J. Richard, *The Founders and the Classics*, 50.
8   On slaves in art, see N. Himmelmann, *Archäologisches zum Problem der griechischen Sklaverei* (Wiesbaden: Verlag der Akademie der Wissenschaften un der Literatur, 1971)
9   *Antiphon and Andokides*, trans. by M. Gagarin and D.M. MacDowell, vol. 1,

The Oratory of Classical Greece (Austin, Texas: University of Texas Press, 1998)

10 James C. Scott, *Domination and the Arts of Resistance: Hidden Transcripts* (New Haven: Yale University Press, 1990)

11 Aristophanes, *Wasps*, trans. J. Henderson (Newburyport, Mass.: Focus, 2008)

12 See P. duBois, *Torture and Truth* (New York and London: Routledge, 1991); Michael Gagarin, 'The Torture of Slaves in Athenian Law,' *Classical Philology* 91 (1996), 1–18)

13 'Andromache,' trans. J.F. Nims, in *Euripides* vol. III, ed. D. Grene and R. Lattimore (Chicago: University of Chicago Press, 1958)

14 Joseph Vogt, *Ancient Slavery and the Ideal of Man*, trans. T. Wiedemann (Oxford: Basil Blackwell, 1974), 75. Vogt cites Posidonius fragment 35 in Jacoby *F. Gr. Hist*=Athenaeus 6, 272e-f)

15 Brent D. Shaw, trans. and ed., *Spartacus and the Slave Wars, A Brief History with Documents* (Boston: Bedford/St. Martin's, 2001), 55. Shaw here cites P. Berlin Leihg., 15. This volume is an invaluable source for information on slavery, slave revolts, and Spartacus' rebellion.

16 Herodas, *The Mimes and Fragments*, with notes by Walter Headlam, ed. A.D. Knox (Cambridge: Cambridge University Press, 1966), xlv.

17 Keith Bradley, *Slavery and Rebellion in the Roman World, 140 B.C.-70 B.C.* (Bloomington and Indianapolis: Indiana University Press, 1998), 18.

18 Shaw, p. 71.

19 On the plays of Menander, see Susan Lape, *Reproducing Athens: Meander's Comedy, Democratic Culture, and the Hellenistic City* (Princeton: Princeton University Press, 2004)

20 Kathleen McCarthy, *Slaves, Masters, and the Art of Authority in Plautine Comedy* (Princeton: Princeton University Press, 2000), 212

21 Terence, *The Comedies*, trans. B. Radice (Harmondsworth: Penguin, 1976), 71.

22 William Fitzgerald, *Slaves and the Roman Literary Imagination* (Cambridge: Cambridge University Press, 2000), 11.

23 Kathleen McCarthy, '*Servitium Amoris: Amor Servitii*,' in *Women and Slaves in Greco-Roman Culture: Differential Equations*, ed. Sheila Murnaghan and Sandra R. Joshel (New York and London: Routledge, 1998), 174–192; passage cited, 182.

24 Cicero, *Selected Letters*, trans. D.R. Shackleton-Bailey (Harmondsworth: Penguin, 1982), 109, #39.

25 Keith Hopkins, *Conquerors and Slaves: Sociological Studies in Roman History*, vol. 1 (Cambridge: Cambridge University Press, 1978), 118

26 Horace, *The Complete Odes and Epodes with the Centennial Hymn*, trans. W.G. Shepherd (Harmondsworth: Penguin, 1983), 102

27 P.R.C. Weaver, *Familia Caesaris: A Social Study of the Emperor's Freedmen and Slaves* (Cambridge: Cambridge University Press, 1972)

28 Suetonius, *The Twelve Caesars*, trans. Robert Graves (Harmondsworth: Penguin, 1957)

29 Juvenal, *The Sixteen Satires*, trans. Peter Green (Baltimore: Penguin, 1967), 68.

30 Martial, *The Epigrams*, trans. J. Michie (Harmondsworth: Penguin, 1978), p. 51

31 Cited in Garnsey, p. 213

Chapter 5

1   G.M.S. Dann and A.V. Seaton, eds., *Slavery, Contested Heritage and Thanatourism* (Binghamton, New York: Haworth Press, 2001), co-published as *International Journal of Hospitality & Tourism Administration* 2 (2001)

2   S. Fjellman, *Vinyl Leaves: Walt Disney World and America* (Boulder, Colorado: Westview Press), 1992.

3   G.M.S. Dann and R.B. Potter, 'Supplanting the Planters: Hawking Heritage in Barbados,' in Slavery, Contested Heritage and Thanatourism, 51–84; passage cited, 56

4   Patience Essah, 'Slavery, Heritage and Tourism in Ghana,' in *Slavery, Contested Heritage and Thanatourism*, 31–49; passage cited, 47

5   Gilles Deleuze, *Cinema 1: The Movement-Image*, trans. Hugh Tomlinson and Barbara Habberjam (London: Continuum, 1986 [1983]), 148

6   *Plutarch's Lives*, trans. John Dryden, rev. A. Clough (New York: Modern Library, no date), 655

7   See Mary Beard, *The Roman Triumph* (Cambridge, Mass.: Harvard University Press, 2007), 265)

8   Cited in Shaw, 143–4

9   Shaw, 14

10   This legacy is explored in:

11   Martin Winkler, ed., *Sparticus : Film and History* (Oxford: Blackwell, 2007)

12   Maria Wyke, *Projecting the Past: Ancient Rome, Cinema, and History* (New York and London: Routledge, 1997)

13   *Gladiator: The Making of the Ridley Scott Epic*, introduction by Ridley Scott (New York: Newmarket Press, 2000), 7, 11.

14   Cited by Jon Solomon in '*Gladiator* from Screenplay to Screen,' in Martin Winkler, ed., *Gladiator: Film and History* (Oxford: Blackwell, 2004), 1–15; passage cited, 5

15   Peter W. Rose, 'The Politics of *Gladiator*,' in the same volume, 150–172; passage cited, 172

16   Carlin A. Barton, *Sorrows of the Ancient Romans: The Gladiator and the Monster* (Princeton: Princeton University Press, 1993)

17   On the politics of the film see Monica S. Cyrino, '*Gladiator* and Contemporary American Society,' in *Gladiator: Film and History*, ed. Martin Winkler, 124–149. Cyrino notes a parallel with contemporary concerns about the collapse of the nuclear family, athletics as spectacle, and the exhaustion of empire.

18   Arthur J. Pomeroy, 'The Vision of a Fascist Rome in *Gladiator*,' in Winkler, ed., 111–123; passage cited, 121.

19   Martin Winkler, '*Gladiator* and the Traditions of Historical Cinema,' in Winkler, ed., *Gladiator: Film and History*, 16–30; passage cited, 25

20   *Herodian*, vol. 1, trans. C.R. Whitaker (Cambridge, Mass.: Harvard University Press [Loeb Classical Library], 1969)

INDEX